BERLITZ

HAWAII

By the staff of Berlitz Guides

Library of Congress Catalog Card Number:
79-91849.

Berlitz Trademark Reg. U.S. Patent Office
and other countries – Marca Registrada.

Printed in Switzerland by Weber S.A., Bienne.

12th edition (1992/1993)

Updated or revised 1992, 1990, 1989, 1986,
1985, 1984, 1983, 1982

How to use our guide

- All the practical information, hints and tips that you will need before and during the trip start on page 107.

- For general background, see the sections Hawaii and the Hawaiians, p. 6, and A Brief History, p. 14.

- All the sights to see are listed between pages 30 and 87. Our ![i] own choice of sights most highly recommended is pinpointed by the Berlitz traveler symbol.

- Entertainment, nightlife and all other leisure activities are described between pages 87 to 102, while information on restaurants and cuisine is to be found on pages 103 to 106.

- Finally, there is an index at the back of the book, pp. 126–128.

Found an error or an omission in this Berlitz Guide? Or a change or new feature we should know about? Our editor would be happy to hear from you, and a postcard would do. Be sure to include your name and address, since in appreciation for a useful suggestion, we'd like to send you a travel guide. Write to: Berlitz Publishing Company Ltd., London Road, Wheatley, Oxford OX9 1YR, England.

Although we make every effort to ensure the accuracy of all the information in this book, changes occur incessantly. We cannot therefore take responsibility for facts, prices, addresses and circumstances in general that are constantly subject to alteration.

Text: Jack Altman
Photography: Kurt Ammann
Layout: Doris Haldemann
We are most grateful to Anne Harpham for her help in the preparation of this book. We also wish to thank the Hawaii Visitors Bureau, in particular Lindy Boyes, for their valuable assistance.
4 Cartography: 𝕱𝕒𝕝𝕜 Falk-Verlag, Hamburg.

Contents

Photo, pp. 2-3: Polynesian Cultural Center, Oahu

Hawaii and the Hawaiians

The best—and first—thing you can do with your watch in Hawaii is to put it away in your suitcase. Time is of no great importance 2,000 miles from anywhere else, in a paradise of year-round sunshine, relieved by the breeze of a trade wind. What's time when you're living amid a dramatic landscape of volcanoes and the bluest of blue oceans—settings so grandiose as to be, quite literally, breathtaking?

In the middle of the North Pacific—and not the South

Pacific, as many romantics and movie-goers might imagine —this 50th state of the U.S.A. is an archipelago of seven inhabited islands (one reserved for the Navy) a collection of islets, reefs, sandbars and rocks strung out in an arc over 1,500 miles from South Point on the "Big Island" of Hawaii in the southeast to the little dot of the Kure Atoll in the northwest. The Hawaiian Islands are the peaks of a mountain range raised from the bed

Exotic beauty in land of contrasts: rare silversword plant on volcano's brink, and city-bred Hawaiian belle.

of the ocean by a series of volcanic eruptions some 25 million years ago. Those volcanoes, a couple of them still active, have created a richly varied country: towering cliffs, old craters now overgrown with fern and trees, plunging waterfalls, barren cinder cones amid eerie moonscapes and, at the island shores, crags of rock spewed up from the earth's core, and the pulverised jet black sands that make an impressive contrast with the more familiar, dazzling white beaches and their comforting whispering palms.

The state's capital, Honolulu, is on the island of Oahu. The island of Hawaii, locally known as the Big Island to avoid confusion with the state name, is well over twice the size of all the other islands put together but has only a tenth of Oahu's population. Oahu is the busy island, the island with the densest population, the most traffic, the most commerce. It's the island that the U.S. Armed Forces have chosen as their command post for the Pacific, Far East and Southeast Asia. It's also the most popular island for tourists. Swimmers and just plain sunbathers love its long white beaches—though by that same token they are scarcely ever peaceful. Surfers, that hardy breed of sun- and sea-worshippers who are Hawaii's special sporting gift to the world, still swear that the perfect wave is more likely to be found on Oahu's north shore than anywhere else on earth. And when the sun's gone down, Waikiki offers the islands' most vigorous nightlife.

The Big Island of Hawaii has enormous contrasts. Its two great volcanoes, Mauna Kea and Mauna Loa, have snow on their peaks four or five months of the year, while the near-desert of Ka'u is permanently hot and arid. To the east the island's main town, Hilo, is known as the City of Rainbows, a pleasant, very Hawaiian way of saying it gets a lot of rain—very good for its lovely orchids and the nearby waterfalls—while the Kona Coast, the west coast around Kailua, is as sunny as anyone could hope for. But the Big Island's main feature remains its volcanoes and one of them, the Kilauea Crater, is safely observable, even though alive with the hiss of escaping steam, a sniff of sulphur and even an occasional glowing eruption—all under

There are secluded beaches to be found everywhere. Lumahai Beach lies on the north side of Kauai.

the cautious supervision of government observatories.

Maui is fast becoming as popular as Oahu—though without Oahu's almost metropolitan resort atmosphere in Waikiki. One of Maui's great charms is the old royal capital and subsequent whaling town of Lahaina. Now boats go out not to hunt but to view these delightful mammals, the humpback whales, that swim the island's warm western waters in the winter and early spring-time. North of Lahaina is a luxuriously developed resort area with superb golf courses and tennis courts and lovely beaches. Maui's mountain, the 10,000-foot Haleakala, has a paved road right to its summit where its dormant volcano crater is both an awesome landscape and a living geography

Honolulu harbor offers the total Hawaiian picture of skyscrapers, palm trees, sailboats, catamarans . . .

lesson in how clouds form and dissipate at your very feet.

Somewhat less romantic, off Maui's southwest coast, is the uninhabited island of Kahoolawe—formerly used by the U.S. Navy and Air Force for target practice.

Further north, Molokai and Lanai are less visited than the other islands but that, for many people, is their prime asset. Both are restfully quiet and splendid for rugged jeep-trips or long hikes and—best of all, say the adepts—mule-treks along the cliffs, mountain trails and through the forests.

Kauai, the northernmost of the inhabited islands, is also the greenest and justly known as the Garden Island. Its lush vegetation is fed by some of the few real rivers to be found on the islands, a delight for trout-fishing. The valleys abound in waterfalls and the grandiose Waimea Canyon has nothing to fear from Mark Twain's comparing it to Arizona's Grand Canyon. The soaring Na Pali cliffs, accessible to boats, helicopters and only the most persevering hikers, are not easily compared to anything.

Last but not least, Kauai's neighbor island, Niihau, remains the state's most mysterious. It is privately owned by the Robinson family and only a couple of hundred Hawaiians of Polynesian origin living there are allowed on it. These Hawaiians of Niihau have a special source of pride: they live in much the same fashion as their ancestors did.

As an isolated island culture, Hawaiians in general have made a big thing out of who was a *kama'aina*, literally "child of the land" and so a long-time Hawaii resident, and who was a *malihini*, a newcomer or visitor. It's all a question of historical perspective. Today any resident of Hawaii considers himself or herself a *kama'aina*, reserving the word *malihini* for tourists. Even among tourists, those who've been to Hawaii before start thinking of themselves as *kama'aina*, leaving the first-timers as the only questionable *malihini*. But among the Hawaiian residents themselves, the Hawaiians of Polynesian origin consider themselves the only true *kama'aina* and all others—Europeans, Japanese, Chinese, Koreans or Filipinos—are in the scheme of things all newcomers, *malihini*. The Niihau residents, having avoided intermarriage with other peoples on the islands, consider themselves the absolute élite of *kama'aina*.

Hawaii at its best is a serene playground for adults and chil- **11**

Hula dancers wear a lot more clothes these days than they did in the 19th century when missionaries imposed stringent laws on decency.

dren. The people enjoy life and can't bear the idea of having anyone around who doesn't. Their smile is not just contagious, it's almost a law of the land. When they hang a *lei* around your neck, it's still more often made of real rather than plastic orchids. You receive it **12** graciously with a kiss and you're welcomed to the brotherhood of smile. At the traditional feasts known as *luaus*, those smiles are as sweet and pervasive as the pineapples in the cuisine. If you come from a meteorologically or emotionally cold climate, you may be tempted to view all this sunny cheerfulness as artificial and commercially

motivated. But you'll soon find that even the most dedicated public relations efforts at the airport and the hotels have been unable to submerge the real friendliness and sincere hospitality that are the mark of the beautiful Hawaiian hinterland. They greet you with their famous "Aloha" and they're not just saying "Hello". It's a word meaning love, peace, good will, a wish of general wellbeing that sets the ideal tone for their relationships. Ideal, because it's not always possible in metropolitan Honolulu or in an expressway traffic jam, but it remains the Hawaiian goal.

The ethnic mix has known its times of conflict and hostility, but by and large the interracial harmony of Hawaii is the most successful in the U.S., perhaps because everybody is part of a minority group. The original Hawaiians of Polynesian ancestry and part-Hawaiians now make up about 18 percent of the population. European ancestry accounts for the islands' largest group, but still less than 30 percent, just ahead of the Japanese. Intermarriage is becoming the rule rather than the exception.

You're bound to notice the importance so many Hawaiians attach to physical fitness. Elsewhere in the world, jogging may be a passing craze. In Hawaii it's a way of life, like breakfast or cleaning your teeth. No one wears a lot of clothing so people are a little more conscious of their bodies. They want to look and feel good. And the chances are that you, too, will unconsciously "loosen up", find yourself taking on more relaxed attitudes, habits, frames of mind... That's when you know you've caught "aloha spirit". Hawaii has claimed another happy victim.

13

A Brief History

The Hawaiian Islands were always a dream destination, even for Polynesians. The name itself in Polynesian referred to a homeland for departed souls. The sturdy seafaring people who spread out across the Pacific from the Asian mainland via the Malay peninsula and Indonesia edged their way ever further east, to Samoa, Tahiti and the Marquesas, and heard from returning fishermen that there was still one more as yet uninhabited Garden of Eden to conquer to the north.

Archaeological evidence is scanty, but it suggests that around A.D. 750 and perhaps as early as 400 the first settlers arrived in Hawaii from the Marquesas. This voyage of over 2,000 miles was probably undertaken in ocean-going 100-foot dugout canoes with outriggers or double-hulled catamarans, with sail woven from coconut fibre. (Boats of the same basic design can still be seen around Hawaii today—with fibreglass hulls and nylon sails.)

The only animals there to meet these first settlers were the tiny Hawaiian bat and perhaps the monk seal, said by zoologists to be the only mammals indigenous to Hawaii. The Polynesians brought their own chickens, pigs and dogs (the latter as food, not pets) and breadfruit, bananas, yams, sugar cane and *taro*, the starchy root crop central to the Polynesian diet.

Between 1200 and 1400, with the arrival of a tougher breed of men from Tahiti to dominate the gentler Marquesan pio-

neers, Hawaiian society developed a feudal character. Strong chief-kings governed by their own physical prowess together with the divine support of priestly advisors who operated as prime ministers. One tribe ruled each of the four largest islands—Hawaii, Maui, Oahu and Kauai—while little Molokai and Lanai had to pay costly tribute to one or other of them and provide battlegrounds for the interisland warfare. The chiefs owned all the land and enforced their authority with an

Defeated soldiers sought sanctuary with gods of this city of refuge.

elaborate and rigid system of taboos (*kapu* in Hawaiian).

But life in Hawaii was also a lot of fun with swimming-races, surfing—on four-yard long surfboards—boxing, wrestling, bowling, darts, tobogganing on grass. And the people loved music, singing to gourd-drums (ukuleles didn't appear until the Portuguese arrived in the 19th century) and dancing the *hula* at the drop of a skirt—the clothed version being post-missionary.

Captain Cook

Britain's Captain James Cook was first to report to the world his fateful "discovery" of the islands in 1778, naming them the Sandwich Islands after his patron, the Earl of Sandwich, First Lord of the Admiralty. Actually Cook's ships, the *Resolution* and the *Discovery*, had been looking for a sea-passage between the Pacific and the Atlantic—subsequently provided by the Panama Canal—and stumbled on the islands as a welcome haven to stock up with pork, fish and sweet potatoes. In exchange, the Hawaiians who sailed out to the ships off Kauai received brass medals, iron nails and venereal disease. The hot item was the iron nails. Just one moderate-sized nail could be traded for a whole day's pork.

All the ships' metal became a great target for theft.

Later, Cook paid a visit to the island of Hawaii, and in February 1779 at Kealakekua Bay (marked today by a memorial statue south of Kailua), was welcomed ashore as Lono, God of the Harvest, and feasted with great ceremony. But the thefts of the ships' ironware continued and Cook tried to stop it by kidnapping the main chief of Hawaii, Kalaniopuu. On his way back to ship, Cook, considered to be acting in a most ungodlike manner, was stabbed by angry natives and hacked to pieces. For burial, the British were given only a few bones of Cook's body, the rest being either burned or distributed among the chiefs for ritual sharing in the great man's strength.

Kamehameha the Great

Captain Cook's hair was especially coveted, and the man who got it became Hawaii's most illustrious leader—Kamehameha—uniting the islands and becoming their first king in 1795.

Even previously, when he became chief of the Big Island in 1779 at the age of 30, he was already renowned for his physical strength, demonstrated in peacetime exhibition fights. These consisted of single-hand-

Captain Cook arrived in 1778 and life was never the same again.

ed combat or mock pitched battles, often to the death, with the chiefs dressed in a cloak and helmet made up of hundreds of thousands of red and yellow bird-feathers and fighting with spear and stone-sling.

Kamehameha got control of the islands by winning the arms race unleashed by European and American fur-traders seeking stores on their way to the Chinese markets at Canton. Hawaiian chiefs were tough bargainers and sold their prized hogs only for guns and ammunition. Kamehameha's great triumph was to commandeer, by guile and brute force, the schooner *Fair American*, complete with guns and cannon and two seamen, Isaac Davis and John Young, to run it for him. With this he was able to invade Maui and gain control of Oahu, Molokai and Lanai as well. Only distant Kauai eluded him until the last part of his reign, in 1810. The wars were brutal, fought on sea and land, in the bottleneck Waipio Valley on Hawaii and on the Nuuanu Pali cliffs on Oahu—where hundreds jumped to their deaths rather than submit to Kamehameha's retribution. **17**

But the foreigners' guns caused less deaths than their cholera, typhoid and even measles, against which the isolated Hawaiians had no resistance. Cook had made a survey that indicated a population of around 300,000 in 1778. By 1820 it had dropped to 135,000.

Kamehameha's best foreign friend was Captain George Vancouver, who had served as midshipman under Cook. The Hawaiian king loved to hear how things were done by his counterpart in London. He proceeded to set up a monarchic government, unique in the Pacific, modeled on Great Britain.

Kamehameha cannily combined the trappings and structure of British monarchic government with traditional Hawaiian customs to maintain tribal solidarity. A viceroy or governor was appointed to each island and authority asserted by flag, fanfare and parade. But the old religious customs were maintained at the *heiau* temples, where the *makahiki* harvest festivals were the high point.

King Kamehameha won control of Hawaiian islands when he won the arms race for European cannons.

Seeking the skills of carpenters, navigators, sailmakers, blacksmiths and gunsmiths, the king encouraged foreigners to settle, though he was less happy about the refugees from the British prison colony at Botany Bay, Australia. His favorites were given land and "went native" with two or three wives at a time. One American, Oliver Holmes, became the boss of Honolulu* trade, kept 180 servants and gave banquets of barbecued dog. The Spanish linguist and adventurer Don Francisco de Paula Marín was the paramour of many female chiefs and cultivated a vineyard and gardens on an island at Puuloa (Pearl Harbor).

Fashionable Hawaiians tattooed on their arms such exotic names as William Pitt, Thomas Jefferson and Napoleon Bonaparte. They invited Americans to join their Fourth of July celebrations with rockets and fireworks in the royal yam patch. Always great gamesmen, the Hawaiians became no mean poker-players and beat the sailors mercilessly at checkers (draughts), which they found to be a tame variation of their own *konane*, played—still—with black and white pebbles.

Revenue—in barter and hard cash—came from hogs, fruit, vegetables, firewood, salt and drinking water. There was a lucrative but short-lived boom in sandalwood for the Chinese market. The king took his due on pimping Hawaiian women to the sailors. But this practice perversely gave women a means of overcoming their historical subservience and Kamehameha's carefully maintained system of control by' taboo began to crumble. He died in 1819 at Kailua on the Big Island and his bones were buried in secret so that no successor should draw on the *mana* of Hawaii's greatest king.

He was succeeded by his 22-year-old son Liholiho (King Kamehameha II), but the real ruler of the kingdom was the favorite of his 21 wives, Kaahumanu, who served as regent and prime minister. This strong-willed, heavy-drinking woman broke down the taboos against women eating pork or shark's meat. Six months after his death the taboos had virtually all disappeared—just in time for the arrival of Christian missionaries from Massachusetts.

---

* It was an English merchant captain, William Brown, who in 1792 found and established the harbor of Honolulu, the only place with a navigable channel through the coral reef, protected anchorage and water deep enough to take up to 100 ships close to shore.

19

Missionary Time

Two ordained ministers, Hiram Bingham from Vermont and Asa Thurston from Massachusetts, both strict Calvinist Congregationalists, arrived in 1820 with a farmer, two teachers, a doctor, a printer—essential for the propaganda effort—and their wives. Until two months before their departure, all had been bachelors except the farmer. Brides were hurriedly rounded up for them so that they would not be diverted from their mission which Bingham said was "to train for heaven" a people filled with "unrighteousness, fornication, wickedness, murder, debate (sic), deceit, malignity".

But Liholiho and Kaahumanu had rejected the old religion because of its repressiveness and didn't like the idea of picking up another one so quickly. The young king had five wives, two of whom were inherited from his father, and another was his half-sister. He didn't enjoy the missionaries' disapproval of the Hawaiians' apparent lackadaisical attitude to work, of the "lewd dancing" of the *hula*, their public nakedness, the king's polygamy and incest.

The American mission made slow progress until Kaahumanu was nursed back to health by Bingham's wife after a long illness. Her conversion was sudden and drastic; not only did she attend church and mission school but cut a swathe through the islands' *heiau* temples, burning the carved images of the old gods. Liholiho found the whole thing very boring, opting instead for a life of luxury amid silks and satins and a lot of alcohol. The only thing he liked about the missionaries was their New England furniture and Old English china, using only the finest for his banquets—while reclining naked on straw mats. The old Hawaii had not yet disappeared.

In 1824 Liholiho went on a trip to England with his queen, Kamamalu, to see his "friend" King George IV, not knowing the latter had told his Foreign Office he wanted no contact with this "pair of damned cannibals". George was saved the trouble because the Hawaiian royal couple caught measles in London and died before their appointed audience. Back in Hawaii their deaths were regarded as punishment for their sinful lives—Church recruitment rose sharply.

With the heir to the throne a mere child, Kaahumanu was the undisputed ruler, a boon to the missionaries. Their biggest obstacle was not so much the paganism of the Hawaiians as the dissolute opposition of the merchants and sailors on shore leave (Governor Boki of Oahu was getting $1 a head for each woman going aboard ship). At the urging of Bingham, Kaahumanu banned prostitution, which started riotous street battles between English sailors and missionary helpers at Lahaina.

The Ten Commandments were proposed as the basis for a Hawaiian Constitution. Resistance to the idea was led by Boki, who had accompanied Liholiho to London and seen how that great Christian capital had worked with prostitution and other vices. Supported by the merchants and sailors, Boki was also joined by the British and American consuls, both embittered diplomatic career failures who hated missionary moralizing. To calm matters down, the Hawaiian authorities drew up a fundamental moral law proscribing murder, theft and adultery and, in deference to non-missionary whites, reserving prostitution, gambling and the sale of alcohol for a later date. When Boki died in 1831, Kaahumanu replaced him with her 300-pound brother, who sent out a police force around Honolulu to stop alcohol sales, gambling, billiards, bowling, dancing, even riding.

The great missionary success was undoubtedly the schools, with 50,000 pupils, mostly adults, learning to read from Christian textbooks printed locally in Hawaiian. Exams were Hawaiian-style celebrations—conch shells were blown to summon the pupils dressed up in ceremonial robes, evergreen wreaths on their heads and red and yellow *leis* around their necks.

When the grand old lady Kaahumanu died, the missionaries lost their great ally. Eighteen-year-old King Kauikeaouli (Kamehameha III), a pupil of Governor Boki and already a great philanderer, was certainly no Christian. He lifted penalties on prostitution, adultery and all other crimes except theft and murder. The missionaries were horrified by his love affair with his sister, during which he tried to commit suicide when they stopped its consummation. He let the other chiefs rule in his name and withdrew to a relatively quiet life of sailing, riding, bowling and billiards with his foreign merchant and sailor friends.

In 1840 Bingham was forced by his wife's illness to return to New England and the missionaries abandoned hope of total victory for Puritanism, opting instead for more pragmatic **21** compromise. Mark Twain observed on his visit to the islands: "Sin no longer flourishes in name, only in reality."

American Ascendancy

Pragmatic compromise moved the missionaries from the spiritual to the squarely secular world. The missionaries had been sent to Hawaii with strict instructions not to intervene in local politics. With morality like everything else in life ruled by politics, this proved to be impossible. But whereas Bingham's first wave of missionaries took no official post, preferring to perform as grey eminences behind the throne, the next wave, led by physician-missionary Gerrit P. Judd, stepped out in front. Judd was variously finance, foreign and prime minister and often all three at once. He loved the trappings of power even more than old Kamehameha, wearing gold crowns on his coat, sitting in the royal pew in church, riding in a

The Hawaiian Flag

The flag of the USA's 50th state includes the British Union Jack; this oddity stems from a whim of King Kamehameha, the British flag being a gift from his pal Captain Vancouver which he flew in front of his various island residences as a tribute to the admired customs of his fellow monarch. It was first hoisted in 1795, to shouts of "We are men of Britain!"—a popular sentiment of the times, when the chief of Kauai called himself King George—although there was never any formal political link. In 1816, eight red, white and blue stripes were added, for each of the main islands, assimilating the style of the American flag. A sentimental link with Britain remained even after American annexation of 1898 and incorporation as a state in 1959. Queen Elizabeth was startled to see her flag flying at Honolulu Airport when she passed through on her way to Australia in 1963. She was assured (and reassured) this was not a mislaid bit of her Empire, and given a Hawaiian flag as a memento.

On Molokai the clapboard steepled houses enjoy a life of simplicity far, far from the madding crowd.

gilded, brocaded coach and ordering 17-gun salutes for his arrivals and departures at official events. King Kauikeaouli didn't understand all the fuss—he said he'd rather be captain of an ocean-going clipper.

In the 1840's, the king's foreign advisors organized for him the *Great Mahele* or Land Redistribution. Previously each island governor had owned all the land, giving away only a few choice parcels to court favorites. Now, in the interests of democracy, the land was to be redistributed to Hawaiian commoners and leased to foreigners. The complexities of land-ownership and sale baffled Hawaiian royalty and commoners alike, and foreigners obtained land at rock-bottom prices, mostly for the islands' first large-scale sugar plantations. Boundaries in valleys had previously been fixed by rolling a stone down; now they were set by triangulating surveys. Landmarks like streams, trees and rocks were replaced by lines and dots on maps. Hawaiian commoners confronted with the intricacies of freehold tenure preferred to sell off all their land—to foreigners who understood such things. By the end of the 19th century, they owned four times as much land as Hawaiians. The island of Niihau was bought outright by the Scottish family Robinson for $10,000.

While Americans were definitely in the ascendancy, asserting their entrepreneurial genius, the British and French affirmed their presence with their own time-honored asset– the gunboat. In 1843 British imperial might was called in to back the local consul's private land-grievances. Six years later, the French brought in their big guns to reinforce their consul's complaints about trade-discrimination. The ventures were more insulting than dangerous, but enough to send Judd to Washington to seek American protection. He even tried to sell the islands to New York millionaire Alfred Benson for $5,000,000. The first talk of annexation began, but Washington was reluctant to get involved and, a decade before the Civil War, most Americans on the islands opposed the idea because it might lead to statehood, which would give Hawaiians equal rights as U.S. citizens. The Hawaiian leaders exploited this feeling to defeat the annexation movement by insisting on a statehood-clause, guaranteeing its rejection in the U.S. Congress.

These were tumultuous times. Sailors rioted in Honolulu over Judd's draconian puritanical restrictions. In 1853 a smallpox epidemic killed between 2,500 and 5,000, nearly all Hawaiians who were reluctant to take the vaccine and frightened by reports of autopsies—carving up bodies in ways alien to their old funeral traditions. The turmoil, administrative disarray and financial scandal caused the dismissal of Judd. The next year Kauikeaouli died and his heir, Prince Alexander Liholiho, who had led the anti-annexation movement, took the title of Kamehameha IV.

Wine, Women and Whales

Court life under the new king imitated the pomp of Napoleon III's Second Empire—buxom princesses in plunging necklines dancing till dawn, their beaux frittering away fortunes on wine—all demonstrated the decline of missionary influence. The more ceremonious Episcopalian Church gained at the expense of the austere Low Church Congregationalism. Lower down the social scale the same spirit prevailed in the dance-halls, brothels and bars of Honolulu and Lahaina, greatly favored by the whaling-boat crews.

Spending $10 a head, 12,000 sailors coming through Hawaii

in a good season brought $120,000 in revenue—$100,000 of it in prostitution. Thus the brothels were a major source of income, but also a constant breeding ground for disease.

Whales, long a source of riches, are now simply museum pieces.

Whaling had begun modestly in the 1820's, rose to a record 600 boats docking in Hawaii in 1846 and maintained a steady 500 a year in the 1850's. Its decline began with the discovery in 1859 of oil in Pennsylvania, replacing whale-blubber for oil-lamps. The American Civil War brought the trade almost to a halt and the death blow came in 1871 when 33 ships were trapped and destroyed in the Arctic ice-floes.

But the Civil War also destroyed sugar sales from the southern to the northern states and the Hawaiian sugar industry came into its own. Exports rose from 1,500,000 pounds in 1860 to 17,750,000 in 1866. With island investments switching from whaling to sugar, Hawaii sought a trade agreement with the U.S. that would guarantee its sugar duty-free sales on the American market. Hawaii learned the American golden rule that you get nothing for nothing: in return for the sugar trade privileges, Washington let it be known it would one day demand Pearl Harbor for its navy.

Newcomers

The new prosperity from sugar brought with it the need for more cheap labor. Hawaiians didn't enjoy the back-breaking **25** work, and American plantation-owners were unhappy with productivity. The first Chinese workers were brought to the islands in 1852. They were followed by Portuguese from the Azores and Madeira and by Japanese. They were hardworking, but the Portuguese proved to be uncomfortably ambitious to buy land of their own and the Japanese aroused distrust with their strong, self-sufficient community.

A new constitution organized the vote by property qualification, admitting more Americans to political power. Native Hawaiians became increasingly discontented with these foreign incursions. A small revolt erupted briefly on the Kona Coast of the Big Island. King Kalakaua, who came to the throne in 1874, exploited the racial tensions to Hawaiian advantage. He fixed elections with well-tried European and American methods—lavish pre-election *luaus* for the natives, gin at the ballot box and his own brawny "poll-watchers" to ensure that the royal list would be elected.

Meanwhile a new scourge hit the islands—leprosy, killing hundreds of Hawaiians, who called it *mai pake*, "the Chinese disease", though its real origins remained a mystery. A colony of 1,000 lepers was established on the north coast of Molokai.

Like Kamehameha the Great, King Kalakaua liked to surround himself with exotic foreign adventurers. The Italian Celso Cesare Moreno arrived aboard a Chinese coolie boat. He spoke 12 languages and offered $50 to each Hawaiian legislator to vote him an opium license and a steamship service to haul coolies from China. The royal valet was a German named Robert, or, as he preferred, Baron von Oehlhoffen, who accompanied Kalakaua on a world tour in 1881. Consulting nobody, Kalakaua proposed a Pacific Confederation to the Emperor of Japan. He met the King of Siam, the Khedive of Egypt, Pope Leo XIII, Queen Victoria and Gladstone and came home with new ideas about monarchy.

He built a new Iolani Palace in Honolulu and staged a grand Napoleonic coronation in which he wore Kamehameha's great feather cloak and put the crown on his own head. The celebrations lasted two weeks, with fireworks, canoe regattas, horse-racing and—rescued from 60 years of missionary anathema—*hula*-dancing. He may have admired Europe but Kalakaua was a resolute champion of Hawaiian custom.

He was supported in this by William Murray Gibson, another mad adventurer, an American who made and lost a fortune running guns in the Caribbean, became a Mormon and claimed he was the abandoned son of an English lord. Gibson set up a Mormon colony of converted Hawaiians on Lanai and then moved to Honolulu to wangle his way up to the Prime Ministership. He sold Kalakaua on the idea of reigning over a Polynesian Confederacy covering the whole Pacific in opposition to European and American colonization, and even fitted out an old guano-trader as a gunboat to carry the idea to Samoa. The enterprise collapsed in chaos and international indifference.

Alarmed by Kalakaua's extravagant adventures, the scions of two old American missionary families, Sanford Dole and Asa Thurston, organized the Hawaiian League, backed by vigilantes known as the Honolulu Rifles. An opium-trading scandal in which Kalakaua had apparently accepted a large bribe from a Chinese merchant provided the excuse for revolutionary action. The king was forced to sign a document reducing him to a constitutional monarch. He was stripped of his powers over the armed forces; the Navy and native Hawaiian board of health were abolished. The property qualifications of the Reform Constitution excluded two out of three Hawaiian voters. The days of Hawaiian independence were numbered. It was 1887. To ensure the sugar privileges, Pearl Harbor was ceded to the U.S. for its exclusive use as a naval station, against Kalakaua's wishes.

Annexation

Sapped by a century of debilitating exposure to this strange, demanding Western civilization, Hawaiians put up little resistance. Robert Wilcox, one of several half-Hawaiians taken by the Italian Celso Cesare Moreno to Italy for a European education, came back with dreams of being the Hawaiian Garibaldi. Boldly he led his red-shirted Liberal Patriotic Association against the Reform Constitution, but with little more than fiercely incoherent rhetoric. His armed rebellion was put down but political skirmishing continued. The Reform Cabinet had tried to get Kalakaua to abdicate in favor of his sister Liliuokalani. A conscientious Christian and composer of the beautiful, lilting song *Aloha Oe*, she was expected to be more malleable. Once **27**

Queen, after her brother's death in 1891, she put up a tough struggle for the waning powers of the Hawaiian monarchy.

Fearing she would overthrow the Reform Constitution with a coup d'état, Dole and Thurston invited the U.S. Navy to land its troops at Honolulu. Queen Liliuokalani was forced to surrender. The Provisional Government which replaced her monarchy in 1894 sought U.S. annexation, but President Grover Cleveland disapproved of its action and it had to be content with declaring itself a Republic, not coincidentally on July 4. Sanford Dole was named President.

The growth of Japanese imperialism in the Pacific persuaded the U.S. that Hawaii might after all be a useful acquisition as a bastion against further Japanese expansion. The Senate approved annexation in 1898 and Dole changed his title to Governor.

As a Territory, Hawaii went through many tense moments before achieving full statehood. Ironically it was to be the Japanese on the islands who would finally convince a jittery Congress that Hawaii was a safe bet for admission to the Union. By 1920 they numbered 120,000, mostly plantation workers (compared to only 18,000 Americans and less than 60,000 native Hawaiians) with loyalties as strongly bound to Japan as the Americans felt for the U.S. This was a major obstacle to Hawaii's statehood, particularly with the growing war threats in the Pacific, even though the new generation of Japanese in the 1930's were switching their allegiance to the

Arizona Memorial pays tribute to the war dead of Pearl Harbor.

28

U.S. All attempts to show that the Japanese represented no threat in Hawaii were shattered by the bombing (see p. 38) of Pearl Harbor in December 1941. The war changed all.

World War Two

With Japanese residents at first suspected as spies and enemy collaborators, Hawaii was placed under martial law for almost all of World War Two. In fact 1,400 arrests were made, including Japanese consular officials and some Italians and Germans, all sent to the American mainland for internment. The 160,000 other Japanese were mostly badly needed skilled workers who immediately proved their American loyalties. Kimonos and sandals were put away, private clubs closed down and the older generation stepped up attendance at English classes. The Japanese-language press and radio were censored but in general conditions were much better than in Cali-

fornia with its "relocation camps".

The young Japanese called themselves AJA's (Americans of Japanese Ancestry) and volunteered for the U.S. Army. About 3,000 of them were shipped around the U.S. to avoid risk of activity subversive to the war-effort, but by June 1944, these Japanese Americans were fighting at Civitavecchia and Rome as part of the U.S. Army 100th Battalion and continued fighting throughout Italy and France. The loyalty of Hawaiians, Japanese or otherwise, was never again questioned and the postwar drive to statehood began. After years of political jockeying with Alaska (admitted as the 49th state in 1958), Hawaii finally gained full statehood March 12, 1959.

With Congressmen, Senators and Governors of Chinese, Japanese and even American extraction, Hawaii has offered the Union a 50th State of surpassing mellowness. After years of conflict, it became clear that, although Hawaii has certainly been Americanized, the much more striking development has been to see how Americans—and any other settlers on these smiling islands—have been unmistakably Hawaiianized. The final victory is **30** Hawaii's.

Where to Go

Oahu
(population 836,000)

Oahu is the island for the young at heart who need to boogie... and for all the others who just need a rest. The old Hawaiian name means "the gathering place", conferred long before tourism became Hawaii's biggest industry and made of this island a teeming mecca for sun- and surf-fanatics.

With over 75 percent of the state's total population, Oahu has the islands' only real metropolis, Honolulu (400,000 inhabitants), founded to serve the ocean-going ships using its natural harbor, and now the seat of state government, commerce and industry. For all the criticism of the island's commercialization, one boon should be noticed: the total lack, here and elsewhere in Hawaii, of any advertising billboards along the road, banned by ordinance since the early part of the century.

Two mountain ranges—the 3,000-foot Koolau and the 4,000-foot Waianae—tower along the eastern and western coasts. Between the two ranges lie the sugar and pineapple plantations and the U.S. military bases that occupy one quarter of Oahu. (There are also banana fields, but unlike pineapple and sugar, bananas are for local consumption only. Nobody has felt the urge to turn them into an industry.) Tucked between the sea and the mountains are small residential communities whose residents commute in hordes across the island to work in Honolulu. You'll notice the houses built up on stilts, against flooding and ter-mites. The north and south coasts are beach-country, Waimea mostly for surfers, and Waikiki mainly for sun-bathers.

So much for general orientation, but you'll find once you're traveling around the island that north, south, east and west lose their normal value for directions. Residents prefer to talk of

The last rays of the setting sun outline double-hulled catamaran gliding off east coast of Oahu.

OAHU

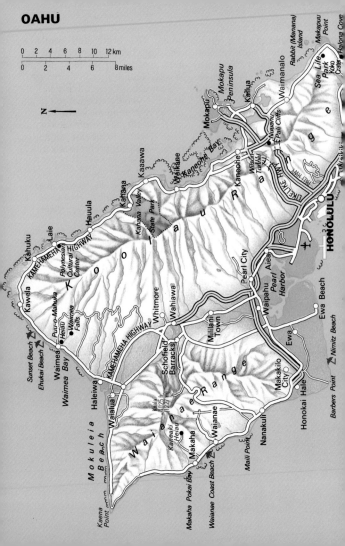

places being *mauka*—toward the mountains, inland—or *makai*—toward the sea—in relation to where you may be standing. On the move, you will be told to go *ewa* (pronounced "eva"), toward the Ewa Plantation west of Honolulu and by extension north-west, or "diamondhead", toward the Diamond Head crater east of Honolulu and by extension to the south.

At first look, **Honolulu** seems much like any other large American city, full of skyscrapers, shopping centers, parking lots and traffic jams. What exotic Polynesian or Oriental touches you might note are most often very evidently American pastiches. But the palm-trees and scarlet hibiscus and the variegated colors of the citizenry's clothing soon make it clear that you are not anywhere but Hawaii.

There are three buildings you should definitely visit to recapture something of Hawaii's past (for hours, see p. 123). **Iolani Palace,** at King and Richards Streets, is the perfect reminder of the whimsical career of the Hawaiian monarchy. Built in 1882 by King Kalakaua, its imposing Victorian-Florentine architecture emphasizes the impression made on the king by the tour he made of the Old World's great cities one year earlier. Nobody has been able to explain why it is almost an exact replica of the Athens home of the great German archaeologist Heinrich Schliemann, excavator of Troy. Queen Liliuokalani was held in the palace under house-arrest for nine months while Hawaii was turned from monarchy into republic on its way to becoming an American territory.

The **Mission Houses Museum,** at 553 South King Street, encompasses the original homes and workshops of the first American missionaries. Well restored, these are the ear-

---

Quizzing Cook

Who got there first, coconuts or Captain Cook? In its splendid isolation, Hawaii was the most virgin of territories, and one of the most intriguing exhibits in the Bishop Museum is an illustrated quiz to test your knowledge or rather your ability to guess when various animals and plants arrived—before or after the Polynesians, before or after Captain Cook? A Hoary Bat, for instance, and the lovely silversword tree ferns were there before anyone. But coconuts and sugar arrived with the Polynesians. Pineapples, goats and mosquitoes came after Cook.

liest American structures in Hawaii, prefabricated white wooden frame houses shipped from Boston around Cape Horn in 1821. They served as home and school for over 100 years. The two coral block buildings beside them housed the mission stores and the all-important printing press (of which a working replica can still be seen) that produced the Bible and hymn books to spread the good word in Hawaiian.

For the best overall view of the islands' history, visit the excellent **Bishop Museum,** at 1355 Kalihi Street, founded in 1889 as a memorial to Princess Bernice Pauahi Bishop, last direct descendant of the Kamehameha line of Hawaiian chiefs. The museum, with three splendid interior galleries of indigenous dark *koa* wood, traces the Hawaiian heritage from its Polynesian beginnings, with examples of the canoes used to colonize the islands and the artifacts which the Asians,

Europeans and Americans have contributed to the multiracial present.

You can see the old *koa*-wood surfboards, measuring up to 14 feet 6 inches, the marvelous red and yellow royal feathercloaks and *leis*, carved wood and stone gods and models of temples where human sacrifices were performed. There is a fine collection of Polynesian artifacts from all over the Pacific. The centerpiece of the museum is a 55-foot-long skeleton of a sperm whale that weighed more than 20 tons live.

Seekers of the seedy-exotic might enjoy a trip to what is left of **Chinatown.** It successfully survived a devastating fire in its 100-year history but is having a harder time with urban renewal. Commerce thrives on Maunakea Street and honky-tonks on Hotel Street. The seediest of all are the bars down at the waterfront, but definitely worth a look for the truly adventurous, perhaps those who remember with affection

Two monuments of Honolulu's Victorian past: Iolani Palace and the Falls of Clyde cargo vessel.

Pruitt's escapades in James Jones' *From Here to Eternity*.

A more stately attraction on the waterfront is the **Falls of Clyde,** a four-masted museum ship at Pier 7. Built in the Clyde shipyards of Scotland in 1878, it served as a cargo vessel, passenger ship and oil tanker in the Pacific until 1959.

Before you hunker down to the serious business of Operation Suntan, you should make your pilgrimage, dutiful for some, fascinating for all with a sense of history, to **Pearl Harbor** (see also box on p. 38). Free tours are organized by the U.S. Navy, with a visit to the floating memorial over the wreck of the *Arizona.* The longer, paid commercial cruises from Kewalo Basin to Pearl Harbor do not include a visit to the memorial. Each has informative guides giving commentaries, but there is considerably more charm to the patriotic accounts of the cadets employed by the Navy,

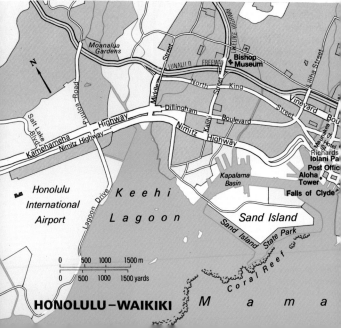

HONOLULU–WAIKIKI

expressing special pride in the new fleet of nuclear submarines moored across from the old Battleship Row. Tours start with an introductory film explaining the historical background—how the Japanese felt prompted to attack because the U.S. Pacific Fleet represented a barrier to Japanese access to the strategically important oil supplies of Southeast Asia.

One of the eerie aspects of a tour of the old battle area is the oil-slick you can see to this day seeping up from the hundreds of tons of oil still stored in the holds of the sunken *Arizona*.

The Hawaiians of old had always tended to avoid Honolulu, disliking its muddy shores and hot humid climate; they preferred the beaches further east, at Waikiki, with its cool coconut grove and white sands, the perfect place for a holiday, even 200 years ago. Today, in the hit-parades of celebrity status, **Waikiki** is in constant competition with Miami Beach, Atlantic

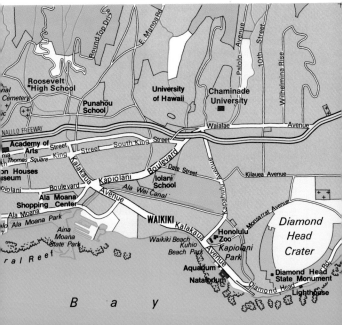

Pearl Harbor

Late in 1941, the F.B.I. told Washington the Japanese consulate in Honolulu was burning its files. The breaking of Japanese diplomatic codes alerted the U.S. to the threat of "Operation East Wind Rain" mounting an attack somewhere in the Pacific. They found out exactly where at 7:55 a.m. on Sunday, December 7, when most of the U.S. Navy's Pacific Fleet was still sleeping soundly after a night out on the town. The Japanese had closely studied American sailors' weekend habits in Honolulu. Pearl Harbor was practically defenseless when the first bombs fell.

Battleship Row, off Ford Island, had eight ships at anchor. The Japanese mission chief Fuchida confidently sent back his code signal for success "Tora, Tora, Tora" (tiger, tiger, tiger), two minutes *before* dropping the first bombs. The military band on the *Nevada* had started up the "Star Spangled Banner" for the 8 a.m. flag-raising as the torpedoes were speeding on their way.

Oklahoma turned upside down. *West Virginia* and *California* sank. *Tennessee* and *Maryland* were seriously damaged. The flagship *Pennsylvania* was blasted onto its side in dry dock. *Arizona* blew up and sank with 1,100 crew aboard. *Nevada* was the only ship able to get under way and avoid further damage. The U.S. Army and Navy had 402 planes compared to Japan's 360, but only a tiny fraction of the American planes got aloft. U.S. casualties were 3,435, Japanese less than 100.

After the war a report to Congress said: "The astoundingly disproportionate extent of losses marks the greatest military and naval disaster in our Nation's history."

City and Malibu for the title of America's best-known, best-loved and therefore most maligned sea resort. The hotels, restaurants and shops cater to a popular clientèle and are unashamedly extrovert in appeal. You can roll right out of your hotel bed into the sea—though many people seem to prefer the swimming pools that even the beachside hotels provide for their more cautious guests. Waikiki may be guilty of some noise-pollution and visual assault in its more garish high-rise architecture, but tourism is too important an industry for the Hawaiian Chamber of Commerce to allow the seawater to get polluted. For a tour of the area, board the tourist trolley that shuttles between Hilo Hattie Warehouse, the Ala Moana Shopping Center and the Royal Hawaiian Center at the start of Waikiki Beach.

Waikiki—where it's all at.

Waikiki Beach is 2½ miles long and one of its best sections is **Kuhio Beach Park,** well-sheltered for safe swimming. You can rent surfboards and take graded lessons for Waikiki's surfing equivalent of nursery ski-slopes before venturing out to more challenging stuff, especially round to the north side of the island and the big waves of Waimea.

At the far eastern end of Waikiki looms **Diamond Head,** an extinct volcanic crater where sailors in the 19th century found some calcite crystals they mistook for diamonds. The Hawaiians called it Leahi, after the yellowfin tuna whose forehead the ridge seemed to resemble. The 760-foot high crater rim is best viewed from the beach but scarcely worth the rough scramble if you are going on to visit the more spectacular volcanoes on the Big Island of Hawaii or Maui. What is worth a visit is the **Waikiki Aquarium** in Kapiolani Park, *ewa* (west) of Diamond Head, for its superbly displayed collection of Pacific sea-life.

If you drive on eastward past Diamond Head, you'll pass between two more extinct craters, KOKO HEAD to the south and KOKO CRATER to the north. At the foot of Koko Head is the romantic **Hanauma Bay,** with the beach where Burt Lancaster and Deborah Kerr had their torrid love scene in the film *From Here to Eternity.*

At MAKAPUU POINT is **Sea Life Park,** which cleverly makes oceanography a supremely entertaining branch of show business. Its Hawaiian Reef Tank, with 300,000 gallons of constantly changing ocean water, takes you on a spiral tour of over 2,000 different specimens of marine life. It's absolutely hypnotizing to descend and stare right into the cold, cold eyes of a hammerhead shark and walk on in a trance to come face to

Who's Fooling Whom?

Animal-lovers sometimes find the relationship between trainer and dolphin a little patronizing, but it's not always clear which of the two is being patronized. For instance, rewarded with a fish after each trick, one particularly prolific dolphin at Sea Life Park had soon eaten its fill but, because it liked playing, it continued to accept the fish and stacked them uneaten at the bottom of the tank. Then, when finally tired of playing, the dolphin fetched up one of its spare fish and… gave it to the trainer as a reward.

face with a nasty moray eel. When it shows you its sharp little teeth, it isn't smiling, just regretting the glass pane between the two of you. But there are also the charming butterfly-fish and the yellow-beaked parrot-fish. The spines of the fragile-looking lion-fish are especially lovely and poisonous.

The Park's biggest attractions are the Ocean Science Theater and Whaler's Cove, where bottlenose dolphins and whales perform spectacular acrobatics separately and in unison 22 feet through *hula* hoops and 17 feet up to the yardarm of a model whaling-

It's often hard to tell who's getting most fun, the dolphins or their oceanographer trainers.

boat. They are coached with loving care and great humor by trained oceanographers who assure the public, ever more alert to ecological exploitation, that these oceanic mammals really enjoy the fun and games as a normal part of their regular activities. It is true that if you travel around the islands, particularly off Maui, you may spot dolphins and whales performing, quite naturally, some of the tricks coordinated at Sea Life Park. **41**

When you're on your way to the northern side of the island from Honolulu, take the Pali Highway which goes through a tunnel toward the towns of KAILUA and KANEOHE. Just before the tunnel there is a well-marked exit up to the **Nuuanu Pali Lookout.** Follow it. It's "just" a view, but a terrific view, well worth the detour—a sheer 1,000-foot drop down a cliff at a breach in the Koolau Mountains. The view is best enjoyed not from the concrete observation platform but from a railing a little further below. Hold on tight because the Trade Wind rushes through the gap in the mountain ridge. It was over this cliff that Kamehameha drove his enemies in his 1795 conquest of Oahu as part of his effort to unite the Hawaiian Islands into one kingdom.

Time and again, Oahu's scenery presents contrasts of rustic calm and a strange primeval wilderness.

Whether, as some say, he pushed them or they preferred to jump, the fact is that hundreds ended up on the rocks below, their bones serving as souvenirs for travelers till the end of the 19th century.

On very rare occasions you may see the only wild life of the Oahu mountains—a couple of wild boar. Incidentally, there's nothing to worry about underfoot when hiking around—not a single snake on any of the islands.

The northeast coast road, known locally as the Kam (-ehameha) Highway, goes past some pleasant beach parks on its way up to LAIE and the **Polynesian Cultural Center,** operated by the Mormons of the Brigham Young University–Hawaii. Here you can tour "villages" of the Pacific people, with representative housing and craftwork of Fiji, Samoa, Maori New Zealand, Tonga, the Marquesas and old Hawaii. In slightly homogenized form,

there's a river-pageant on canoes, evening performances of music and dance in native costume. You can learn the proper way to break open a coconut and extract its milk—not the juice in the middle but the liquid scraped and squeezed from the white meat of the nut. British visitors will be astounded—and Americans doubtless delighted—to see what happened to the sedate English game of cricket once the Samoans got hold of it, with the players applauding, cheering and booing, thumping on kerosene drums and blowing police-whistles. From the Maori you can learn the rhythm of swinging and slapping the double-strung *poi (taro)* balls.

Skirt the northern tip of the island and you will reach the fabled surfing areas of **Sunset Beach,** Banzai Pipeline at **Ehukai Beach** and **Waimea.** Even if you are not up to participating (see p. 87), you will want to see, on waves that break 35 feet high in winter, the golden and shining copper gods and goddesses of the supreme Hawaiian sport, performing feats of grace and daring to thrill the most lethargic of landlubbers. Waimea Bay is particularly lovely and worth a picnic in the park. Take the electric tram trip up to the 55-foot Waimea Falls.

While in the area, look for the red-and-yellow marker of the Hawaiian Visitors Bureau (used for all the islands' important monuments) indicating the **Puu-o-Mahuka Heiau.** This temple, which has a fine view of Waimea Bay, was the site of human sacrifices, including that of three Englishmen of Captain George Vancouver's crew in 1794. You may also find new sacred *ti* leaves—signs that the old beliefs have not died out—placed under rocks to propitiate the gods. Locals will tell you that it is not just the Hawaiians of Polynesian extraction who place these holy leaf-offerings. This place somehow does something to you.

Another temple that deserves a visit if you find yourself on the west coast by MAKAHA is the carefully restored **Kaneaki Heiau,** just off the Makaha golf course. Built of volcanic rocks at various stages between 1450 and 1640, it was at first an agricultural temple for worship to enhance the harvests. You can see the stone platforms on which the god-images were assembled, the wooden tower for the priests, a drum-house and stone altars for sacrifices. After 1750 it became a war temple and was probably used by Kamehameha during his conquest of Oahu.

Hawaii—
The Big Island

(population 120,000)

Until the European and American sailors arrived and the demands of their ocean-going ships moved the main focus of attention to Oahu, the island of Hawaii was the historic, cultural and political center for all the islands. As the home of Pele, the volcano goddess who created the islands, and the birthplace of their greatest king, Kamehameha, it was natural that this island would bear the name for the whole archipelago. Symbolically it was also appropriate that the island of Hawaii saw the death of Captain Cook, the man who opened up the territory to Europeans and Americans and the subsequent shift of power to Oahu.

More than twice as big as all the other islands put together, today it is content to be known simply as the Big Island. And almost visibly happy that Oahu is stuck with the hustle and bustle of metropolitan life—"almost" because, although for the visitor the island's tranquillity

Liliuokalani Gardens are just one place where Japanese have left a graceful mark of their identity.

is delightfully restful, the Big Islanders themselves are sometimes wistful about the lost economic opportunities, especially around the sugar plantations of the North Kohala coastal region, abandoned because of the concentration of power in Oahu. But, in the end, everyone settles back to enjoy the special peace of the Big Island, its spectacular volcanic landscapes of Mauna Kea, Mauna Loa and Kilauea, which Apollo astronauts studied in preparation for their walks on the moon; the refreshingly cool climate on the eastern Hamakua Coast, north of Hilo; and the guaranteed sun of the western Kona Coast around Kailua.

The island is particularly proud of its flowers, boasting several thousand varieties of exotic blooms in its gardens, nurseries and growing wild. The Big Island provides most of the orchids that make up the *leis* hung around your neck in Honolulu and elsewhere. As you drive around the island, you'll notice the bright red *lehua* blossoms on the *ohia* trees. Lehua was said to be a princess in love with the commoner, Ohia, and a kindhearted god brought them together as blossom and tree. Pick the flower, say the Hawaiians, and it will rain the tears of Lehua at

being parted from her beloved Ohia. On the Big Island, around Hilo, they're constantly in need of explanations for the sudden rains. Public relations geniuses thought of calling them "liquid sunshine". But they really shouldn't worry. Rain, here as anywhere else in the islands, is not something to upset you or make you grab for an umbrella or even a raincoat. It rarely sets in for a whole day and is to be thanked for the gorgeous flora. After a few days of unadulterated sunshine, you'll be praying for the liquid kind as refreshment.

The island's capital, **Hilo**, is the rainiest of Hawaii's towns, with 136 inches a year—five times as much as at Waikiki (or Kailua-Kona, on the other side of the island). But this fact also makes it the greenest and most colorful of the state's towns. Draped around a bay, it offers just east of Sampan Harbor the Japanese-style **Liliuokalani Gardens,** complete with pagodas and stone bridges, one of them leading over to Coconut Island, the perfect place for picnics. In Sampan Harbor itself is the **Suisan Fish Market** with its lively auction-bidding in Pidgin English starting around 7:30 a.m. every day except Sunday. Around town you can look at the myriad orchids in various

46

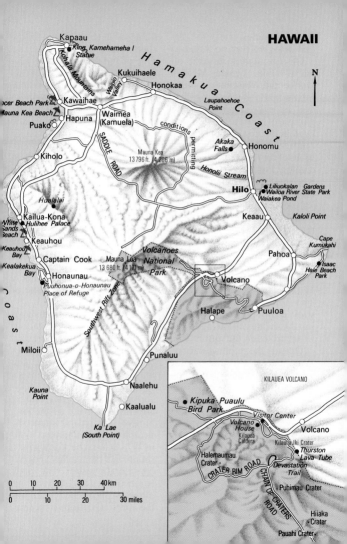

HAWAII

N

Kapaau
King Kamehameha I
Statue

Kohala Mountains

Hamakua Coast

Kukuihaele
Honokaa
Waipio Valley

Laupahoehoe Point

Spencer Beach Park
Mauna Kea Beach
Kawaihae
Hapuna
Puako

Waimea
(Kamuela)

conditions permitting

Akaka Falls

Honomu

SADDLE ROAD

Kiholo

Mauna Kea
13 796 ft. (4,206 m)

Honolii Stream

Hilo

Liliuokalani Gardens
Wailoa River State Park
Waiakea Pond

Hualalai

Kailua-Kona
Hulihee Palace
White Sands Beach
Keauhou
Keauhou Bay

Keaau

Kaloli Point

Cape Kumukahi

Captain Cook
Mauna Loa
13 680 ft. (4,171 m)

Volcanoes National Park

Pahoa

Isaac Hale Beach Park

Kealakekua Bay
Honaunau
Puuhonua-o-Honaunau
Place of Refuge

Volcano

Southwest Rift Zone

Halape

Puuloa

Coast

Miloii

Punaluu

Kauna Point

Naalehu

Kaalualu

Ka Lae
(South Point)

0	10	20	30	40 km
0	10	20	30 miles	

KILAUEA VOLCANO

Kipuka Puaulu
Bird Park

Visitor Center

Volcano House
Kilauea Caldera

Volcano

Kilauea Iki Crater

Halemaumau Crater

CRATER RIM ROAD

Thurston Lava Tube

Devastation Trail

Puhimau Crater

CHAIN OF CRATERS ROAD

Hiiaka Crater

Pauahi Crater

flower nurseries, one of the biggest being on Hinano Street.

Of considerable historic interest is the **Lyman Mission House and Museum,** as much for its nicely displayed collection of Hawaiiana as for its glimpse of how the missionaries lived in the first half of the 19th century. Among the many exhibits of the foreign settlers—including Portuguese, Filipinos, Koreans and Japanese—the most impressive is a 300-year-old Chinese village Taoist shrine brought to Hawaii from the Wong Leong district of Kwantung. The villagers, emigrating to work in Hawaii's sugar-plantations, disassembled it and brought it piece by piece to Hilo in their personal luggage. The shrine's temple was destroyed by a tidal wave in 1960, but the shrine was salvaged and reassembled in the museum.

Outside the public library on Waianuenue Avenue is the 5,000-pound **Naha Stone.** Whoever could turn this stone over with his bare hands could become king of the islands. Kamehameha did it. Nowadays you simply get elected—kissing babies is less strain on the heart.

The Big Island has many attractive drives, but the best is the tour of the **Hamakua Coast** north of Hilo to Waipio Valley. On the way you will pass many valleys that tempt you to follow them inland to their waterfalls. One of the prettiest is the 420-foot **Akaka Falls.** Ten miles further north, on the other side of the main road, you may want to make your way down to the rough seas at **Laupahoehoe Point,** the site of a devastating tidal wave (see p. 53) in 1946. Carry on past HONOKAA to **Waipio Valley Lookout** and one of the most beautiful views in all of Hawaii. If you have good rubber-soled shoes, hike down the 2,000-foot gorge or take a jeep—there is even a shuttle-service for the less athletic. At any rate, do get off the beaten track for a while to forget civilization in a place that genuinely earns a claim to the name of paradise.

The north coast, **Kohala,** is best known as the birthplace of Kamehameha with his original **statue** at KAPAAU to commemorate the fact. (The one you may have seen in Honolulu is a replica.) This 8½-foot polychrome sculpture has had as adventurous a life as the king himself. Created in Florence by Boston sculptor Thomas Gould in 1878, it has a beckoning pose similar to a Donatello *David* but considerably fatter. The cloak comes down a lot lower over his otherwise naked body than was the carefree custom in Kamehameha's own day. The sculpture was lost at sea when the ship in which it was traveling burned and sank off the Falkland Islands in 1880. Two years later a British captain found the statue standing outside a junk shop in Port Stanley in the Falklands, like a glorified cigar-shop Indian. He took it to Hawaii, where the government bought it back for $875. Though the statue stands proudly at Kamehameha's birth-place, nobody knows

Hilo fishermen bring in the rich catch to Suisan Fish Market, but the vivid flowers smell sweeter.

where the king was buried—a deliberate secret to prevent anybody from drawing on the great man's *mana* by appropriating his bones, teeth or hair.

Coming down the west **Kona Coast** past KAWAIHAE, you will be able to enjoy the island's best beaches—ideal for lazy swimming and sunbathing, the best being **Spencer Beach Park** and **Mauna Kea Beach**. The former is very good for camping, fishing and body- (rather than board-) surfing.

At the village of PUAKO, look out for the **petroglyphs,** the prehistoric rock art of the first Polynesian settlers. To discourage vandalism from casual visitors, these have been left deliberately hard to find, involving a 20-minute trek which locals will point out, but it's well worth the trouble. They are among the best preserved petroglyphs in the islands.

One of the quainter sights of KAILUA-KONA is **Hulihee Palace,** a 19th-century vacation home for the Hawaiian royal family, where you can see in the furnishings—note especially Kalakaua's splendid dining table—the enormous influence of Queen Victoria on the living

Petroglyphs

Hawaiians carved into the volcanic rock primitive but striking pictures of dogs, chickens, turtles and family groups as part of their traditional magic and ritual. These petroglyphs are believed to record journeys and historical events and commemorate legends. You may also find clusters of dots and concentric circles that were probably tallies of population-counts for the tax-collector. Some deeper holes in the rocks were dug to bury the umbilical chord at childbirth to ensure the baby's long life and well-being. Some petroglyphs evidently date from post-1800 as they begin to show European sailboats, anchors, rifles and churches.

style of the Hawaiian monarchy. The family portraits step right out of a House of Hanover photo album—though some of the names are slightly different, for instance Princess Elizabeth Kahaupauokalanikauleleiaiwikalaianole. You can also see the 180-pound stone medicine ball with which Kamehameha is said to have practiced prior to lifting that Naha Stone in Hilo.

South of Kailua is **Kealakekua Bay** where Captain Cook met his death (see p. 16). The white monument is difficult to get to except by boat, but the

You cool down at the first sight of the Big Island's Akaka Falls.

Kapu-breakers

Kapu-breakers—for instance women caught eating forbidden fish or male commoners trespassing on royal property—could escape the punishment of death by running into the sanctuary from the south or swimming into it from the north (to attempt to reach it overland from the north would have entailed the mortal risk of crossing the royal palace grounds). Even Kamehameha's favorite wife, Kaahumanu, had to make use of the sanctuary after a violent quarrel with the king in Kailua. She swam into the refuge and hid under a stone known today as the Kaahumanu Stone. Kamehameha found her there only because her pet dog was seen swimming in after her. No king was strong enough to breach the protective power of the City of Refuge. Kamehameha and Kaahumanu kissed and made up.

site deserves a moment's meditation on the clash of civilizations.

Of all the historical sites dotted around the islands, there's none that gives a more exquisite sense of the Hawaiian experience before the arrival of Europeans and Americans than the **Puuhonua-o-Honaunau City of Refuge,** 4 bumpy miles

south of Kealakekua Bay. If you approach it from the main road, you'll look down 1,500 feet on an oasis of green coconut grove amid an arid wasteland of scrub. This was the sanctuary to which *kapu*- (taboo-) breakers and defeated warriors with their families could flee and find safety and renewed life, absolved by the priests. It is today a national historical park and still the most peaceful of sanctuaries from a world of modern *kapu* and strife.

Built around 1550 at one of the Kona Coast's best fishing areas, it was sanctified by the bones of dead kings and chiefs in a nearby *heiau* (temple). With the advent of Christianity the bones were removed but the holy spirit seems to remain. The king's master stone-masons fashioned huge volcanic rocks, lugged without wheeled transport, to fit together without mortar in a great wall 10 feet high, 17 feet thick and 1,000 feet long, separating the palace grounds from the *puuhonua* (sanctuary). Clamber out over the rocks among the fish pools and you can enjoy the same peace of mind the hustled, beaten soldiers must have felt after a hard day's war.

If you're a collector of geographical landmarks, you'll

want to drive down to **Ka Lae,** or South Point, the southernmost point in the U.S. If not, continue round to **Punaluu,** a dramatic black sand beach resulting from the granulation of volcanic rock by wind and sea. The Big Island's other black sand beach, Kaimu, no longer exists, falling victim to the on-going volcanic eruption.

The highlight of any visit to the island of Hawaii must be the **Volcanoes National Park.** Here you can come into close, safe contact with the whole volcanic process that created the Hawaiian Islands and, indeed, the rest of the earth's solid surface. An excellent Visitor Center is operated by Rangers of the National Park Service; you will be directed to tours and hikes around the major areas of the island's most active volcano, Kilauea. A visit to the geology museum is also worthwhile.

In fact the island has five volcanoes. The northernmost, KOHALA, is extinct. HUALALAI, on the west coast, has erupted once, in 1801. The tallest, MAUNA KEA, 13,790 feet above sea level (though rising more than 30,000 feet from the seabed), last erupted 4,500 years ago but is not yet considered dead. **Mauna Loa,** the "long mountain", 13,670 feet and

Tidal Waves

Actually tidal waves should more properly be called seismic sea waves or more commonly by the Japanese word *tsunami*, since they have nothing to do with the tides. They are an infrequent but recurring phenomenon of Hawaii's natural history, with 34 authenticated *tsunami* from 1813 to 1975. They are caused by displacements in the earth's crust or earthquakes in the sea bed—sometimes as far away as Alaska—with a magnitude of over 6.5 on the Richter scale (Punaluu's even hit 7.2). In 1946 a *tsunami* killed 159 people in Hawaii after an earthquake in the Aleutian Islands. When the earthquake occurs in deep sea, a ship passing directly over the point of the quake would feel nothing more than a wave one or two feet larger than normal. But the waves travel toward the island coasts, building up as the sea becomes shallower and reaching up to 100 feet as they hit exposed land. The *tsunami* that occurred in 1975 caused over $1,500,000 in damage, killing 2 and injuring 19. The U.S. Government has in the meantime set up an elaborate monitoring and early warning system, part of which you can see in the sirens as you drive along the coastal roads.

beautifully snow-capped in winter, erupted in 1975 and is again "inflating". Lava continues to flow sporadically from **Kilauea,** a long, flat, gently sloping "shield" volcano just 4,000 feet high. The overall eruption, which began in 1983, still continues to be alive, and there is action in the lava pond at Pu'u O'o vent.

This eruption destroyed 181 homes as well as various landmarks. The spectacle attracted crowds of sightseeing planes. Even in quiet times there's a 24-hour telephone service (967-7977) by which you can get up-to-date information on the latest eruptions or upcoming attractions. You'll even find temporary

The Devastation Trail outside the Kilauea Crater shows the awesome destructive powers of lava with the regenerative powers of nature.

road signs to guide you to the best vantage points to watch the action.

Only twice in recorded history has Hawaii experienced violent eruptions, in 1790 and 1924, both times at Kilauea, with tremendous explosions of rock, hot mud and poisonous gases, caused by the build-up of great underground steam pressure. More usually, the eruptions are mild releases of slowly moving lava flows, a mere 2,000 degrees Fahrenheit.

Gods and Myths

Hawaii's most feared deity is Pele—daughter of Haumea, the Earth Mother, and Wakea, the Sky Father—the goddess of fire, maker of mountains, melter of rocks, devourer of forests, creator and destroyer. Woman. She arrived first in the island of Niihau, digging her home there in a crater. Na Maka o Kahai, goddess of the sea, drove her out and she moved to Kauai, making a bigger crater-home there. Again the sea-goddess chased her away, to Oahu, to Molokai, to Lanai, to Maui and finally to the island of Hawaii. Here Pele dug her biggest, deepest volcano home, defying the sea-goddess to uproot her once more.

This old myth, in one sweeping gesture, traces exactly the same sequence of the Hawaii Islands' volcanic evolution that latterday geologists have painstakingly reconstructed with years of research.

After some orientation at the Visitor Center and perhaps a snack at the Volcano House overlooking the Kilauea Caldera (a caldera is a broader, shallower crater), start your tour at the **Thurston Lava Tube.** When the lava bursts through the ground like toothpaste from a punctured tube, its outer surface cools and hardens into a crust or roof under which hot liquid lava continues to flow downhill, leaving behind a hollow tunnel, of which the Thurston Lava Tube is a pretty example.

Your next stop should be **Devastation Trail,** which is exactly that, a trail through an *ohia* forest buried in 1959 under as much as 10 feet of pumice and cinders. The eruptions lasted 36 days and destroyed life over 1,250 acres, wherever the lava, cinders or pumice exceeded one inch in thickness. One year later isolated trees miraculously began sprouting leaves again. Now you walk again among the new *ohia* trees producing their red *lehua* blossoms, aided by aerial roots like red beards that breathe in oxygen and moisture for the trees in place of the soil roots suffocated by the lava. Your path is a boardwalk to prevent you unwittingly spreading alien seeds from the soles of your shoes so that botanists can study how plant and tree life recover naturally from volcanic eruptions. At one end of the trail you can peek into the Kilauea Iki Crater created by that 1959 eruption and see geologists still working in silver fireproof uniforms among the spouts of steam from the crater's cracks.

Drive down **Chain of Craters Road** to look at the spectacular chasms and abysses created by other eruptions, notably the Puhimau, Hiiaka and Pauahi craters. Back on the Crater Rim Road that circles Kilauea, stop off at the broad **Halemaumau Crater** for a good whiff of what hell is supposed to smell of—a sulphur that perhaps those with sensitive lungs would prefer to avoid. You can get a good look, without the smell, from the Observatory further north. When all else is quiet, you can always be sure of some action at Halemaumau. Satan never sleeps.

Whatever eerie or nasty thrills you may have experienced around the volcanoes, why not end your trip to the area with a visit to the **Kipuka Puaulu Bird Park,** northwest of the Kilauea Caldera? Particularly on a hot day, you will welcome this haven of greenery, a cool walk through giant *koa* trees and acacias, with an occasional glimpse, or at least the sound, of red cardinals, Chinese thrushes and honeycreepers. You'll notice on felled logs that the trees have no rings to show their age. This is because the climate is so nearly uniform from year to year that annual changes are not marked in their growth.

Maui
(population 91,000)

Maui is the boom island. Its blessed climate, varied landscapes and imaginative resort facilities have made it Hawaii's top attraction over the past few years. In volume of tourist trade, it rivals Oahu and its overloaded Waikiki, and surpasses it in the eyes of many as far as the quality of holiday attractions is concerned. Every imaginable sport is available—horse-riding, golf, tennis, sailing, canoeing and all the watersports—and in a comfortable, unhurried atmosphere.

The people of Maui exude an ineffable self-assurance, more proudly rooted than most in the Hawaiian past, cheerful without being smug about the prosperous present and unperturbed about the future. Some say this blithe attitude derives from the abundance of what experts claim is the world's most powerful marijuana, grown amid the

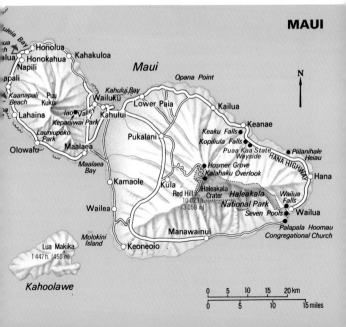

On the Island of Maui, ambiance is such that everyone feels, more or less, that he may be an artist.

sugar cane and in clearings of the dense rain forest and known locally as "Maui Wowie". Others attribute it to a traditional view of the world that goes back to a legend of the island's great demi-god Maui, a kind of Polynesian Hercules or Flash Gordon.

In a story that has sometimes strangely lost in the retelling, Maui's mom once complained the sun didn't shine long enough for her to get her laundry dry. So Maui climbed up Mount Haleakala—"House of the Sun" is the most commonly accepted version—with a rope and lassoed the sun, catching him by the genitals. "Whoa, there!" said Maui, "Slow down!" The sun balked, Maui tightened the noose, the sun relented. Ever since then, Maui seems to be getting more sun than most places—in fact a good 350 days a year—and after a few days on the island you get the feeling the people of Maui could get anything else they wanted, without even tightening the noose.

The carefree attitude is immediately evident in the charming seaport-capital of **Lahaina.**

It became the Hawaiian kingdom's first capital in 1802, after Kamehameha had united the islands, and remained thus until his son moved to Honolulu in 1843. It was perhaps that move that started the fun, for that was the height of the whirling whaling days. The shift of political power probably gave freer rein to the sailors when they came roaring and whoring into Lahaina after long months at sea in the Arctic and Pacific. They fought many a pitched battle with the missionaries and their men for rule of the streets. The missionaries rarely won. Now profanity has settled into a genteel state of goodwill toward all men and women. And Christians go unmolested to the Maria Lanakila Church, around the corner from the missionary **Baldwin House,** now restored as a museum. Only the most malicious readers of James Michener's novel *Hawaii* will see any resemblance between his zealot Abner Hale and the Reverend Dwight Baldwin. Others will enjoy in the decorous home of the Connecticut physician what the Lahaina Restoration Foundation describes as "a fascinating tribute to the New England missionaries who brought to Hawaii the noblest aspects of Western Civilization".

Sheltered from the Trade Winds by the West Maui Mountains, Lahaina is usually slightly muggy downtown. It has the sleepy aspect of an old frontier town with cannily restored pine clapboard façades, pleasant restaurants and inoffensive souvenir shops. Nothing so pleasant as a siesta under the huge spreading century-old Indian **banyan tree** that singly provides shade for a whole park in front of the Court House. The waterfront does colorful justice to the sailboats and catamarans moored for fishing and sightseeing trips.

The whalers have gone, but not the **whales.** From late November to early May, like winter vacationers, the humpbacks come down to the warm Hawaiian waters off Maui and Molokai to frolic around and, more importantly, to mate. Bring your binoculars or cameras and take a cruise beyond Puunoa Point in a glass-bottomed boat for a closer look at the whales, now cherished and protected by the more ecology-conscious descendants of the men who made fortunes from blubber. In Lahaina harbor there's a floating **whaling museum** on a sailing boat named *Carthaginian II* and another up the coast toward Kaanapali, open-air at the Whaler's **59**

Whale Times

Lahaina whale-lovers—it's almost a cult—will tell you more than you might want to know about whales. Here are a few useless facts you might like to trade with them. In evolution whales are cousin to cows and camels. When a whale dives, from head to tail it describes a circle or wheel, from which the Anglo-Saxons took the word for whale. The spout you see coming out of the humpback's blowholes (nostrils) is not water but a cloud of vapor formed by air expelled under great pressure from the whale's lungs and cooling as it emerges. Physiologically, the only important difference between whales and dolphins is size—whales are more than 30 feet long, dolphins are not. Whales and peas have one thing in common—in groups both go around in "pods".

Village Shopping Center, where you can wander around whale-skeletons and the impressive paraphernalia salvaged from the old whaling-ships.

A relic of the town's stormy 19th century can be seen in the reconstructed remnant of the massive coral rock **Fort,** built in 1831 in a vain attempt to withstand the onslaught of the whaling sailors and torn down again in 1854. The masonry was used to build the Hale Paahao Prison, still standing there on Prison Road, of course, for as many of the unruly drunks as could be caught.

If all that is too much like history, take the old sugar-cane train on the Lahaina, Kaanapali and Pacific Railroad out to **Kaanapali Beach** and sleep. Four miles of pellucid sea and clean white sands together put in a tough claim to being the best beaches in Hawaii. And surrounded by two golf courses where the hazards are *ohias* and coconut palms.

Your first inland excursion should be over to Iao Valley, a pleasantly cool state park with more variations on the color green, on its moss and fern-covered mountainsides, than any painter is likely to conjure up from his palette. You'll probably leave from the northern hub of KAHULUI and WAILUKU on the opposite side of the island. The way in takes you through **Kepaniwai Park,** a name meaning "damming of the waters" and referring to the bodies that blocked the Iao Stream after Kamehameha's army had driven Maui's armies into the valley. He slaughtered them with the aid of his new-fangled cannon manned by the two Englishmen, John Young and Isaac Davis. Further along the valley road, Highway 32, you will pass a spot called BLACK GORGE. Stop, and look to the north; you will see at the edge of a ridge halfway up the gorge a natural rock formation eerily presenting a **profile of John Fitzgerald Kennedy.** The Hawaiian islands are full of rock formations which locals claim to resemble Queen-Victoria-lying-down or King-Kong-standing-up—both on Kauai—but none is so stunningly "right" as this one.

Iao Valley itself, the floor of which is 2,250 feet above sea-level, offers a refreshing place for a picnic beside the rushing Kinihapai Stream looking over at the IAO NEEDLE, a 1,200-foot, moss-covered spur. Or else hike up to the waterfalls that build up at the back of the valley, especially in the winter months.

South lies another beautiful valley, WAIKAPU, where the **Maui Plantation** is fast becoming one of the island's most popular attractions. It's a mini-paradise of exotic fruits and flowers, showing how Hawaii's native crops grow and are harvested. A half-hour tram tour takes you around the plantation among fields of sugar, macadamia nuts, guava, passion fruit, coffee, avacado, papaya and much more. Stop by at the complex's own marketplace to purchase some of the produce and souvenir items.

Save for an early morning start your drive up to **Mount Haleakala,** which has a paved road all the way to its 10,023-foot summit. Romantics do. In a state claiming almost as many firsts, biggests and "onlys" as Texas, it must be admitted that there isn't another mountain this high that can be reached by car on an ordinary road. You will, with an early start, witness one of the most beautiful sunrises imaginable breaking across the Haleakala Crater. The sun begins timidly, as if Maui might come back with his lasso, and continues proudly as it climbs out of reach.

The ride through KULA and up the Haleakala Crater Road is in itself a delightful journey around gentle hills, meadows and forests of eucalyptus and pine, the clean sweet air beckoning you at every turn to stop and take a walk. Don't hesitate. The joy of Maui is this ever-changing climate and landscape, from hot tropical sands through rain forest over lush pastures up to Alpine evergreens and ending in the rarefied atmosphere of a desolate moonscape at the **Observatory** on top of the Red Hill Cinder Cone.

From there you look down into a vast crater, or (more expertly) a caldera, that owes its size—7½ miles long and 2½ miles wide—to long-term erosion rather than one original eruption. The crater floor, at its lowest point 3,000 feet below the Observatory, is dotted with cinder cones that oxygen, water and iron have combined to color yellow, red, white, brown, gray and green. In the northeastern corner lies a grassy meadow inside the crater, with

The warriors have borne away the dead and peace reigns over Iao Valley and vast Haleakala Crater.

ferns, forest trees and giant raspberry and holly bushes around the Kapalaoa, Paliku and Holua cabins built for hikers. Yes, you can hike through the crater, and the meadow makes a useful grazing stop for your horse if you choose to ride through. There are marked trails such as the Halemauu from the western side or the Lauulu Trail to Paliku in the east. On horseback, keep to the marked trails so that the horses will not eat the rare plants in the undergrowth.

Come down from the Observatory to the **Visitor Center** for the best view along the length of

all and are tempted to feel a little godlike—until you remember you're just a spectator.

On your way back down the mountain, stop off at the **Kalahaku Overlook** to see the weird and wonderful **silversword fern,** unique to Hawaii and threatened with extinction by the mountain's wild goats and tame tourists. Most tourists obey the federal law posted against picking the silversword but the goats can't read the signs. Further down, there's a fine camp-ground at **Hosmer Grove** with a relaxing nature-walk to change your perspective after the arid volcano crater.

The drive up to Haleakala Crater may be winding but is very easy compared to the rugged craziness of the coastal road from Kahului east to Hana. It's called the **Hana Highway,** but that's only a manner of speaking. No highway 51 miles long should take three hours to drive. Someone once counted 56 one-way bridges and 617 turns but it's not clear he arrived alive: best (and safest) not to count the turns but rather to pause whenever you come to the occasional marked wayside stops. There you can catch your breath and enjoy views of dense rain-forest, with a jungle of creeper coming down to the roadside, or cas-

the crater. If you've arrived in the morning, you can watch the weather "happen", as the Trade Winds drive the clouds up the mountainside and through breaches in the northern ridge, flowing into the crater like rivers and drying out again between the sun and the hot **64** crater floor. You stand above it

cades such as the **Keaku Falls** near the Keanae State Wayside or the **Kopiliula Falls** near the Puaa Kaa State Wayside. It's safe to pick and eat the guava—they're not a threatened species. If you've become a fan of Hawaiian temples, you may want to turn off *makai* (seaward) at KAELEKU to visit the old kingdom's largest, the **Piilanihale Heiau,** but only if you have four-wheel drive.

The panoramas of forest and valleys on one side and the ocean on the other certainly make the arduous drive worthwhile, but the residents at your destination, **Hana,** are delighted that most visitors to Maui find it too much. This makes it easier for the village to keep its name of "heavenly Hana", a place of unspoiled peace and unhurried simplicity which a luxurious resort hotel does not hurt. In addition to its golf course and tennis, the hotel delicately enters into the quiet spirit of Hana by offering croquet. New York, Tokyo and Waikiki are far away.

Hana Bay is a lovely sight and fine for picnics but not so

The Seven Pools on the Hana coast of Maui may not be sacred but they do give people a whale of a time.

good for swimming. It's the gardens of Hana and all along the "highway" south to WAILUA that are clearly the old Hawaiians' proudest possessions, manicured with a care that the most meticulous Englishman must admire. Just past WAILUA FALLS there is good swimming for the adventurous at **Seven Pools,** not sacred as some have claimed, but certainly fascinating for the way the water drains from one pool to another, down finally into the sea.

It was to this part of Maui that Charles A. Lindbergh decided to retire to spend his last days, at peace after his flying exploits around the world. Twelve miles south of Hana you can pay homage to the great aviator in the little seaside **cemetery** of the green and whitewashed Palapala Hoomau Congregational Church he chose for his burial in 1974. His tomb, with its raised volcanic stone platform very much like the sacred platforms of the Hawaiian *heiau,* bears the inscription: "If I take the wings of the morning and dwell in the uttermost parts of the sea…" C.A.L.

Looking out over the Pacific, it is difficult to imagine a more romantic setting in which to spend eternity.

Molokai
(population 6,700)

Molokai has always lived a life apart from the rest of the islands. At first this was because of a fierce tradition of mighty *kahuna* (priests) who spread around them too many *kapu* (taboos) to make life comfortable for the profane. Then, in the 19th century, the long-isolated Hawaiians, with their chronic susceptibility to communicable disease, fell victim in their hundreds to leprosy. With an imperfect understanding of leprosy's causes and care, even after a cure had been found, a panicky Hawaiian legislature bundled the victims out of Honolulu in 1866 and onto boats that left them on an isolated, difficultly accessible peninsula, welded onto Molokai's north coast. Cared for by the Belgian priest Father Damien de Veuster, the lepers formed their own community that gradually became Kalaupapa, the pretty little New-England-style village separated from the outside world only by a mule-track from Kualapuu down the rocky cliffs—and the residual groundless fear born of ignorance. The few remaining lepers, mostly older people living with small pet animals because children are forbidden, have the same serenity and cheerfulness that distinguishes the rest of the island's small population.

Each of the islands has a nickname, but none of them has been more honestly earned by the people—as opposed to being dreamed up by some happy-go-lucky chamber of commerce—than Molokai's "the Friendly Island". Molokai will always be a sleepy backwater, a few nice beaches, a couple of lovely parks, some truly spectacular cliffs and waterfalls (no

Hawaiian island gets away without at least one spectacular view and Molokai's are right up there with the best), but by and large the pleasure of the place is the people. They don't hustle, they don't hurry. They're glad to see a stranger, help him along his way or pass the time of day with him, but they won't automatically try to sell him something. Unless he wants something.

Thus they do not have a big or booming economy.

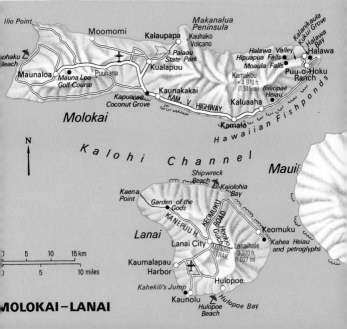

MOLOKAI – LANAI

The pineapple plantations are closing down—they're cheaper in Taiwan—although the pineapple here is delicious. The tourist industry is drowsy. All in all, if you've been island-hopping and are all wired up by the excitements of Oahu, Maui or even the volcanoes of the Big Island, Molokai is the perfect place in which to wind down again and take stock—moon around.

You'll run across a good number of people who came for a holiday and stayed for life. There's an all-in wrestler who retired to go fishing. He's 35. A 40-year-old corporate lawyer from New York who stopped

here to cultivate a garden, and hasn't gone back, a priest who runs a filling-station, an oil-man turned music-teacher. There's an almost painfully apt bumper-sticker you'll see on the rear of cars (on *other* islands), just above the exhaust-pipe: "Wouldn't you rather ride a mule on Molokai?"

The silhouette of Molokai, just 38 miles long and 10 miles wide, is like that of a moccasin, with the toe point east at Halawa and the heel to the west at Papohaku Beach. The flap to the north is the Makanalua Peninsula. There's just one highway, reasonably well paved for two-thirds of its length, running from the toe along the south coast "sole" and then *mauka* (inland) to the old plantation community of MAUNALOA, now practically a ghost town superseded by a golf course.

Start your tour of the island in the middle, at **Palaau State Park,** 234 acres of forest-covered mountainside. The gentle air and hushed silence among the pine trees makes for short walks and long siestas. Rest up for the more challenging hikes you might want to try down at Halawa in the east. The park's big attraction is the Kaule o Nanahoa (Phallic Rock), renowned for its fecund influence on sterile lovers. As a park sign very rightly points out, "phallic rocks are found on all these islands, but this is the finest example". The rock is certainly a vivid enough natural

There are worse things to do than chewing the cud on sunny Molokai. **69**

Rock Power

Kawaluna caught her husband Nanahoa lovingly watching a young girl admiring her reflection in a pool. Kawaluna jealously grabbed the girl by the hair. Miffed, Nanahoa threw his wife over the cliff and she turned to stone on the rocks below. Lusty old Nanahoa turned to stone up in the forest and all his male power remained in the rock, the Phallic Rock, under which women to this day spend the night when they have difficulties getting pregnant. Sometimes they're accompanied by their husbands.

formation to make the most emancipated of women blush and leave the toughest macho roaring with uncomfortable laughter.

At the northern end of the Park is a lovely grass-covered **lookout** over the whole MAKANALUA PENINSULA, its gently rolling surf, wide beaches, and the idyllic setting of the green-roofed houses and gardens of Kalaupapa, 1,600 feet below you. Even if you're not making the hike or mule-trek down to the peninsula, this overview of the old leper colony makes a beautiful introduction to the island as a whole. At the southern end you can see the extinct crater of the KAUHAKO VOLCANO whose eruption spilled several thousand years ago to form the peninsula. If you do make the trek (mules can be rented) down the **Jack London Trail,** make your way to the 405-foot-high crater to get your bearings and look at the same time into the strange blue lake at the bottom. As you wander through the village of **Kalaupapa,** don't miss the **Damien Monument** to the man who gave his life to the colony after it had been virtually abandoned by the rest of the world. On a rock near the monument is the Pidgin English slogan: "Smile—it no break your face".

The north coast from the peninsula to Halawa is open only in part to the hardiest of hikers or jeeps. Otherwise, helicopters (or the plane bringing you to or from Molokai) is your only chance of seeing the marvelous cliffs that protect the coast from human infiltration.

At the west end of the island you'll find some of the best swimming, at **Papohaku Beach,** public but also in large part commandeered by the resort hotel that runs the Maunaloa golf course. If you care to flatter their dining room with your presence, you must change your sandals for proper shoes— which elsewhere in the island is a breach of Molokai etiquette.

While at this end of the island, you might like to see the incongruous **Molokai Ranch Wildlife Park.** Not quite East Africa—the acacia comes from South America and the giraffes resent the difference. Yes, giraffes. The park offers a few hundred acres kept reasonably wild, with salt-licks and waterholes for sable antelope, impala, eland and barbary sheep who all look remarkably healthy. The giraffes just don't seem to like the acacia. One-hour "photo safaris" begin at 7:30 a.m. and 5:30 p.m. only, to give the animals some feeding and sleeping peace in between. No predators, no big cats—the

government won't have them— but it is hoped to add zebra.

The beaches around the island's "capital", KAUNAKAKAI, are better for the all-important siesta than for swimming. But, a mile outside town, you might enjoy a cautious walk through the royal **Kapuaiwa Coconut Grove**—cautious, because all the islands' groves warn you to beware of falling coconuts. One wonders just how the old Hawaiians handled this risk.

On your drive round to Halawa at the eastern toe of the Molokai moccasin, you'll pass some of the old Hawaiian **fishponds,** built between the 15th and 18th centuries to en-

hance the harvest of saltwater fish inside the coral and basalt walls. These fatter fish were strictly for royalty. Commoners got the smaller fry outside the ponds. There were 58 of these ponds along the coast road. At KALUAAHA, the ponds are still in commercial use and successful experiments have been carried out in these and other ponds with clams and oysters.

St. Joseph's Church at KAMALO was built by Father Damien, who took his parish work around the island in addition to his Kalaupapa duties. A couple of miles east of the church, at 234 on the Kamehameha V Highway, is the overgrown path *mauka* (inland) to the **Iliiliopae Heiau** (temple), not easy to find but definitely worth the trouble. This ancient site is on private land but open to the public in small numbers.

The road soon climbs away from the sea north across the Puu-o-Hoku Ranch, claiming the world's largest Charolais cattle herd. (That claim may be defendable and the steak is good, but not *quite* up to Charolais Charolais!) You will also pass the sacred **Kalanikaula Kukui Grove**—candlenut trees

Shopping in Kaunakakai while men harvest sugarcane (previous page).

that sheltered the home of the island's most revered and powerful *kahuna* (priest), Lani-kaula. Such was his hallowed name that the Del Monte pineapple company had to give up the idea of clearing the ground for a plantation because it could not get any Hawaiian workers to cut down the trees.

Drive on down and **Halawa Valley** opens out before you, truly a superb panorama of crashing surf over white sands leading into grasslands back to the jungle of the valley itself. The chasm is divided by two waterfalls, Moaula and Hipua-pua, 3 and 4 miles back. Park your car down by the beach and make at least the shorter hike to the **Moaula Falls.** There and back, it's two hours of sheer joy, through thick banana trees, cool wonders at every turn in the path. The few hikers or campers you're likely to meet—even the odd hermit-resident—will greet you with the most cheerful of smiles; sharing this beauty is like attending the same great party. You can swim in the pool at Moaula but watch out for Mo'o, the legendary lizard that inhabits an underground cave. Test his mood by throwing in a *ti* leaf. If it doesn't float, it means Mo'o would prefer you not to swim that day. Go back to the beach for a picnic.

Lanai
(population 2,400)

The legend of little Lanai, a mere 140 square miles in all, is that for over 1,000 years after the Polynesian settlement of Hawaii nothing lived there except evil spirits. Even when Hawaiians did move in, nothing grew there very well. People scratched a living from their *taro* patches and fished a few fish from the sea. Lanai served as little more than a battle-ground for warring kings from Maui, Oahu and the Big Island. At the beginning of the 19th century, a Chinese entrepreneur tried to start a sugar business but failed. Then descendants of old missionary families bought the island in 1922 and turned the most fertile part of it into one big 18,000-acre pineapple plantation—yes, the world's largest. Christian enterprise triumphed over the evil spirits.

But Lanai is more than just pineapples. It's definitely a good stopover for the robust young hiker, sportsman and four-wheel-drive expert. Although there are only 20 miles of paved roads, the jeep-tracks take you to some exceptional countryside and fine hunting—pronghorn antelope, wild goat, deer, partridge, pheasant—and good game fishing. **73**

Lanai City, scarcely more than a hamlet 1,645 feet above sea-level and surrounded by pine trees, boasts two luxury hotels, the Lodge at Koele and Manele Bay Hotel. The air is refreshingly cool and this may be the one place where you'll need the sweater you forgot to pack. It's also the one place you're likely to enjoy logfires in the evening. For longer stays in Hawaii, Lanai is definitely worth a day or so.

Least visited of all the islands' sights, the landscapes around Lanai are that much less spoiled by construction and as rugged as any romantic could wish. A good start would be the **Garden of the Gods,** out along the Kanepuu Highway northwest from Lanai City. This wild and woolly canyon ought to be the scene for some violent fantasy—Wagner in Polynesia—but you may prefer to enjoy the weird color effects of the sunset, with your head on someone's shoulder. Venture out to **Kaena Point** and muse on the fate of the ladies who were exiled there in 1837 for betraying their husbands in the time-honored manner.

From Lanai City, the Keomuku Road takes you to the north coast. Turn west to **Kaiolohia Bay** and **Shipwreck Beach,** where the squatters' huts

Once the staple crop of Lanai's economy, pineapple is being phased out.

are built from the flotsam of past disasters. The wrecks keep coming in, one disintegrating offshore ever since World War Two, and the coast is good for beachcombing as well as swimming and line-fishing. The eastbound road goes down to the old ghost-town of KEOMUKU where the sugar-plantation failed, the locals say, because the planters took rocks from the nearby Kahea Heiau (temple) to build the railroad. Certainly the **petroglyphs** were sufficient writing on the wall to warn them off.

The south coast is reached by the Manele Road. On the way, try finding the **Luahiwa Petroglyphs** on a small hill east of a turn-off one mile south of Lanai City. It's one of the best collections of old Hawaiian rock art in all the islands, but you'll need the help of a local to guide you to it. You'll see examples of the ancient war canoes with sail and outrigger and more modern drawings of men on horseback, evidently the island's first European visitors.

Some of the most pleasant swimming on the island is to be had at **Hulopoe Bay,** with its beach park for barbecue and picnics, plus a swimming pool for the kids.

One of Kamehameha's favorite stomping grounds was on the southwest tip of the island, at **Kaunolu Village,** now only some evocative ruins. After his conquest of the Hawaiian kingdom, he came

there for rest and recreation, idly fishing while he tested his soldiers' mettle by "asking" them to make **Kahekili's Jump,** marked north of the village. The leap is over a 62-foot cliff into the sea. The "good guys" cleared the 15-foot ledge that juts out just below.

Lanai's best latter-day challenge, for the hiker and jeep-lover, is the **Munro Trail,** a 7-mile dirt road along a high ridge through heavy rain forest up to **Lanaihale,** the island's highest point, 3,370 feet above sea level, with superlative views of all of the other islands except Kauai and Niihau. The trail was planted by New Zealand naturalist George Munro and abounds in the Norfolk pine and other plants that characterize his homeland. On your way up from Lanai City, you'll pass HOOKIO GULCH, scene of a famous battle in 1778. In Hawaii, big battles invariably seem to have ended up at gulches and cliffs, where in the absence of lethal weapons for mass destruction you could always force the enemy to jump. (Hence Kamehameha's training at Kahekili's Jump.) With more peaceful thoughts in mind, save your packed lunch for the Lanaihale summit. It's likely to be just you and an occasional goat.

Kauai

(population 40,000)

Like most places, Hawaii is both a dream and a reality, and if the reality can sometimes undermine the paradise-myth with expressways and highrise condominiums, there is always the island of Kauai to sustain the dream. Kauai is how the romantics *imagine* Hawaii to be. It is known as the "Garden Isle" and Eden is what they have in mind. People move about wide-eyed, as if they hadn't yet touched the forbidden fruit. Oh, they have taken a little bite, but they keep it a secret while they're here. Kauai invites innocence.

Maybe it's the dominant color green—translucent as an emerald, bright as a lime, fresh as an apple, dark as a cucumber and then, when you think you've exhausted the spectrum, a chartreuse green that totally mesmerises you. When you next look in the mirror, you've

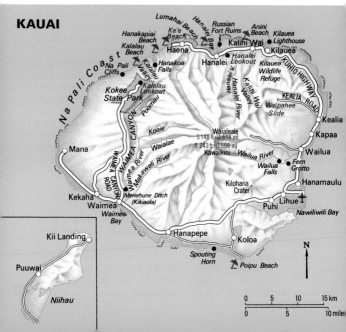

KAUAI

got that wide-eyed look, too. What to call it? The Kauai gaze…?

Kauai has always held itself gently aloof from the other islands. It's the senior partner, first of the volcanic eruptions, eons ago, and geographically separate, 100 miles from Honolulu. With its mysterious private neighbor Niihau, Kauai is the one island that cannot be seen from any of the others. When Kamehameha was conquering the other islands in the 1790's, Kauai stood aghast, awaiting its turn. But Kamehameha never made it across to Kauai. Rather than let his people be subjected to the same bloodshed that had spread over the rest of Hawaii, Kauai's chief Kaumualii, offered in 1810 to submit voluntarily to Kamehameha's suzerainty. In Kauai, anything for a quiet life.

Geographically, Kauai is easy to understand. It was formed by one volcano, Waialeale, which rises in the very middle of the island to its highest point at 5,240 feet. Up there is—yes, this time it *really* is—the wettest area on earth, 471 inches of rain a year. The blessed result of all this rainfall is Hawaii's only real rivers, the Waimea, Makaweli, Hanalei and Wailua. But don't worry, nearly all the rain falls on top of the mountain. The beaches are as sandy as Hawaiian beaches are supposed to be. The warm breezes whisper properly in the coconut palms. The sun is in his heaven and all's right with the world of Kauai.

A good if sometimes winding highway encircles most of the island but mercifully leaves the splendid Na Pali Coast untouched, though that coast can and definitely should be seen by other means, foot, boat or helicopter.

Start where Captain Cook started, 25 miles west of the capital, LIHUE, at **Waimea Bay.** At Cook's Landing, in fact. Sadly, only a feeble little plaque marks the spot where Hawaii's modern history, for good or evil, began with the *Resolution* and *Discovery* anchoring off the sandbanks at the mouth of the Waimea River, on January 19, 1778. Hawaii's contact with Western civilization opened here with an exchange of live pigs and sweet potatoes for some iron nails.

Before following the Waimea River back into the mountain up the spectacular canyon road, take a sidetrip up to the signposted **Menehune Ditch,** also known as the Kikiaola Ditch. This structure has been attributed to apparently mythical but highly controversial little

Hawaii Originals

Hawaiians arguing among themselves as to who are the true *kama'aina* ("child of the land", i.e. aborigine) of the islands often settle the dispute by awarding the title to the Menehune, but most historians dismiss them as pure myth. There are nonetheless some intriguing hints as to their possible real identity. It seems now generally accepted that the Marquesans were the first inhabitants of Hawaii, the Tahitians coming much later and establishing themselves as feudal overlords. In Tahiti, the word for "lower classes" is *manahune*, applied to the laboring plebeians brought from the other Society Islands (same group as Tahiti) and the Marquesas. *Manahune* could be a variation of the Marquesan word *makaainana*, or "people belonging to the land". Perhaps the Menehune were the original Marquesan settlers of Hawaii, put to work as builders by the Tahitians. The legend says some Menehune escaped into the Kauai mountain forests when the Tahitians arrived. In an early 19th century census, King Kaumalii counted 65 Menehune among the 2,000 people of the Wainiha Valley in northern Kauai. Now they appear as commercial symbols in ads for cars and underwear.

folk named the Menehune who, it is supposed, preceded the Polynesians (see opposite). A legend repeated all over Hawaii but most prevalent in Kauai says they were a spirited, hard-working bunch of pygmies, masterful stone masons who worked only at night. If they were unable to complete their construction by dawn, it was left undone. Thus the Menehune were credited with the building of many temples, roads and other structures that couldn't otherwise be accounted for in the Hawaiians' collective historical memory.

Mark Twain, not always the dazzling word-magician, once remarked that **Waimea Canyon** was the Grand Canyon of the Pacific. Arguments about his hyperbole are irrelevant. Waimea is nowhere near as big

Shady coconut groves and long palm-fringed beaches will set even the most blasé a-dreaming.

as the Arizona monster, but its astounding beauty, the freshness of the air and clarity of light are surely unmatched. From the **lookout** at 3,400 feet you may be tempted to watch for hours the play of green in the trees, the ferns, the cactus and the moss, changing with every movement of sun and cloud. Look at the curve of the Waimea River, mountain goats leaping among the rocks, the waterfalls—the pure pleasure of the place will hold you spellbound. There are actually three canyons in the Waimea —the WAIALAE to the east, KOAIE to the north and PO'OMAU to the west.

And that's not all. Up further through the Kokee State Park is the **Kalalau Lookout,** at 4,120 feet the real climax of the drive. Here the panorama over the Kalalau Valley past the HANAKOA FALLS to the Na Pali Coast takes the shape of an amphitheater with the sea as its stage. The Pacific puts on a terrific show. And not a human structure in sight.

It is absolutely not safe for any but the most experienced mountaineer to climb down to the Kalalau Valley. The way into the valley is a fine 18-mile hike along the Na Pali Coast from Haena at the northern end of the island's main highway.

On your way back down the Waimea Canyon Road, stop at the little KOKEE Museum for a nice display of the birds and plant-life of the Canyon and old Hawaiian stone and mother-of-pearl artifacts.

The Canyon Road also gives you a view of the island of **Niihau** to the southwest. The Scottish Robinson family that came via Australia to buy the island in the 19th century still owns it and allows only its 250-odd Hawaiian farmers and fishermen to inhabit it. Operated as one big ranch, it has no electricity, no guns, no jails, no doctors, no alcohol. Strictly *kapu.*

Back in WAIMEA VILLAGE, or rather just outside to the east, take a quick look at the ruins of the **Russian Fort.** Yes, the Russians tried to get in on the Hawaiian act, too. In the very dubious person of a German-born doctor and former Moscow policeman by the name of Georg Anton Schäffer, representing the Russian-American Company in Kauai in 1815. In short, another of Hawaii's special breed of international adventurer. This one tried to corner the coveted sandalwood

Waimea Canyon stretches on out to sea, a million miles from anywhere.

trade for Mother Russia with a few of the islands thrown in, while securing large pieces of choice Kauai real estate for himself. He flew the Russian flag at Waimea but his divided national loyalties could be seen by his renaming of the lovely Hanalei Valley, up in northern Kauai, "Schäffertal". Russia finally disowned him and King Kaumualii chased him out.

Continuing east from Waimea, take the coast road after HANAPEPE to **Spouting Horn.** Watch the waves come rushing up under a ledge of lava on the beach, spouting water high in the air. More dramatic than the Blow Hole in Oahu, this one

makes a sound like an old man's groan after each spout. Further east is the **Poipu Beach** for some excellent, if sometimes crowded, swimming.

There is one hostelry on Kauai which achieves the status of a monument, a crazy monument of Hawaiiana—the **Coco Palms** at Wailua Village.

Even if you don't choose to stay there—and it is by no means the cheapest bargain on the island—you should try to pass by at sunset in time for the amazing nightly **torchlight ceremony.**

Spouting Horn and Coco Palms put on natural and human showbiz.

With the beating of drums and ghostly blowing of conch shells, a disembodied voice intones among the palm trees a homage to the historic Hawaiian past. Lithe Hawaiian torch-bearers clad only in loincloths flit along the banks of a lagoon or paddle by in canoes. For a brief moment the Hawaiian night is aglow with the flaming beacons and a hundred flashes from the visitors' Instamatics.

The Wailua is the only navigable river in all the Islands and you might try to get hold of a private boat or canoe (rather than the crowded, hokey commercial tour-boats) and make your own way up the south branch as far as the trail that leads to the pretty **Fern Grotto.**

Just north of KAPAA, off the Kuhio Highway, is the Kealia Road that takes you to one of the ancient Hawaiians' favorite playgrounds, the **Waipahee Slide,** that used to be frequented by adults and children alike. It's a marvelous natural moss-covered chute over a little waterfall which good swimmers could navigate*. Even for the non-swimmer the pool surrounded by ferns and wild banana plants is a lovely place to take a nap. To get there, follow the road through the sugarcane fields and the left fork away from the irrigation canal to a footpath for a 100-yard walk at the end. There's another, better known but also artificially "improved" waterchute known as the **Slippery Slide** at Kilauea on the north shore. This was built out to avoid the rocks jutting from below during the making of the film *South Pacific* and has remained a popular attraction.

While you're in **Kilauea** visit the Lighthouse and Wildlife Refuge, a bird-sanctuary run by the national parks. The most frequent visitor is the red-footed booby bird. How much of a booby is it? Well, a) it lets its fish-catch be stolen by great frigate birds in mid-air, and b) Spanish sailors used to catch it with their bare hands. That's a booby bird for you.

West of Kilauea is the KALIHI WAI BAY with good swimming at the usually deserted **Anini Beach.**

On your way to HANALEI BAY, be sure to stop at the **Hanalei Valley Lookout,** just after the Princeville Airport, for the superb view back across small farmsteads of *taro*, sugarcane and rice fields to the mountains and the Hanalei River. This side of the island is for society's happy drop-outs.

---

* This slide and the Slippery Slide have **84** been closed owing to accidents.

They have made their homes along this last stretch of road to HAENA. There is popular swimming at **Lumahai Beach,** where Mitzi Gaynor washed that man right out of her hair in *South Pacific.* But the ever-smiling locals prefer going west of Haena to the more secluded **Ke'e Beach** and if they can't find what they want there, they hike to **Hanakapiai Beach.**

Now you're on the **Na Pali Coast** proper and have to decide whether you're up to that 18-mile hike to **Kalalau Valley.** If you have time, provisions and energy, do it. If you can't face the hike, you might consider splurging on one luxury. Go back a few miles to Princeville Airport and take the **helicopter ride.** For 40 glorious minutes or more, Kauai amply repays the expenditure as you swoop along the Na Pali Coast, hop in and out of the Waimea Canyon like one of those mountain goats and then whirl around that rainiest place on earth, Waialeale. You'll be seeing up close places no human being could possibly come near any other way. If Kauai promises a dream, this is one way of fulfilling it.

Aerial view of the Na Pali coast, totally untouched by human hand.

What to Do

Sports

Hawaii is a playground. Playing takes priority over everything, always has, much to the chagrin of the devotees of the work ethic who came after Captain Cook. So throw away your guilt, pick up a surfboard, a tennis racket or some golf clubs and go out and play.

First a word of warning: the sun is a joy but also a killer for the *malihini* (newcomers). The Hawaiian coconut suntan oil can be lethal if you've not already been exposed to the hot sun for some time: it's used by locals to heighten their bronze and is not recommended for the pristine lilywhite. Start out with a protective cream. Anyway, that concentrated coconut smell can be overpowering once you get back to the hotel lobby in the evening; don't add to it unnecessarily.

Surfing

Surfing is the supreme Hawaiian sport and no record exists of it having appeared anywhere else before Captain Cook saw the Hawaiians riding the huge waves off Oahu on long flat boards. He wrote in his **87**

journal: "The boldness and address with which we saw them perform these difficult and dangerous manœuvres was altogether astonishing and scarce to be credited."

Why did the sport develop here? Hawaii's special geographical advantage for surfing was once again its isolation in the huge expanse of water of the North Pacific. With no resistance from other shorelines or landmasses, the winter swells in particular, driven from the Asian continent, hit the northern shores of the Hawaiian Islands with enormous force, unimpeded by a continental shelf. In addition there was probably the simple psychological factor that the Hawaiians' basic playful nature enabled them to see the possibilities of making a sport out of these spectacular surf waves.

At any rate, the ancient Hawaiians developed surfing as an enjoyable but intricate piece of athletic daring and, like everything else in their lives, subjected to feudal distinctions. Commoners used the small, light *alaia* surfboards up to 6 feet in length, designed for all types of surf. Royalty alone was allowed to use the longer—12 to 16 feet—heavy *olo* boards for the larger, longer-breaking surfs. Surfing-prowess was part

of a chief's claim to the respect of his people.

But the 19th-century missionaries regarded surfing as essentially frivolous and discouraged it along with *hula* dancing, so that surfing fell into neglect until it was revived by King Kalakaua in the 1880's. It was given a big boost in 1908 when adopted by young Americans in Honolulu for their newly-formed Outrigger Canoe Club, still proudly in existence at Waikiki, the clubhouse overlooking the best summer surfing on Oahu. Their mentor and surfing champion was the great Hawaiian Olympic swimmer, Duke Pauoa Kahanamoku,

"Surf's up" and away they go— the golden kings of the Pacific.

now practically a patron saint of surfing.

Surfing came into its own at the end of the 1950's and exploded worldwide when the new synthetic foam surfboard was invented and put the sport within comfortable reach of everyone. Traditionally, the best boards had been made of the heavy Hawaiian woods such as *ohia*. Manufacturers had experimented with hollow boards built like airplane wings and used South American balsa wood, coated with fiberglass. A **89**

Surf Talk

Like all serious sports, surfing is lovingly hedged in with an arcane vocabulary all its own. To help you understand a conversation among surfers, here's a quick Berlitz guide to some of the phrases. A surfboard has a "scoop", the upward curving nose that keeps the board above the surface when "catching a wave" or arriving at "take off". The "rocker" is the curve at the tail of the board giving you leverage for turning. The "rails" are the sides and the "deck" is the platform. A wave has a "lip", the top, and a "curl", when the lip begins to fall. The "shoulder" is the portion of the wave that has not yet peaked or become "critical", and the "wall' is the area in which the surfer maneuvers his board. The foam is talked of as "soup" or "white water".

Maneuvers include the "rollercoaster", an acrobatic drive up the face of the wave into the "curl" and dropping back down with the falling water. Getting "tubed" is the great specialty at Oahu's famous Banzai Pipeline, where the wave curls right over the surfer and carries him toward the beach in a tube of water. "Hanging ten" is the act of supreme nonchalance of demonstrating one's masterful stability by walking along the moving surfboard to hang ten toes over the front edge. And then there's the maneuver that everyone can do, the "wipeout", in which you fall off your board. The more advanced version of this is the "bailout", which surfers nicely describe as a "controlled wipeout".

fin or "skeg" was added to act as a keel and the modern surfboard emerged. Today serious surfers have their boards custom-made to obtain the shape and size most appropriate to their weight and preferred style. As a rule of thumb, adolescents should use an 8-foot, women a 9-foot and an average man a 10-foot board. Of course, you can do it without any board at all, just lying on your belly, bodysurfing your way back to the beach.

The best surfing areas in Hawaii vary from season to season and according to your abilities. Consult the experts where you are vacationing, but here's a preliminary guide:

Oahu: *Waikiki* is good for beginners all year; *Chun's Reef* on the north shore is harder. You'll find high summer surf at *Ala Moana, Diamond Head* and *Koko Head.* In the winter, strictly for the experts, the highest waves are at *Sunset Beach, Ehukai Beach* (Banzai Pipeline),

Waimea Bay, Haleiwa and *Makaha*.

Maui: *Lahaina* and *Launiupoko Park* have medium waves. Go to the north shore—*Honokahua, Honolua* and *Mokuleia*—for the bigger waves.

Hawaii: *Honolii* on the Hilo side and *Lyman's Cove* near Kailua have the best all-year-round surfing. *White Sands Beach* and *Hapuna* have nice body-surfing.

Kauai: *Hanalei, Poipu* and *Wailua* all have medium waves.

Surfers go home with their boards like warriors with their shields— but wars just aren't so beautiful.

Other Water Sports

The best **swimming** areas in the islands are usually posted as Beach Parks. You should be on the lookout for areas that have beautiful shorelines but dangerous swimming conditions which change from season to season. These seasonal dangers are usually posted, but when in doubt, ask the locals. On *Oahu*, most of Waikiki is safe all-year-round, but be careful of Koko Head, Makapuu, Halona Cove, Sunset and Waimea. On *Hawaii*, Hapuna Beach is outstanding. Keauhou and Kealakekua Bays have good deep-water swimming. Avoid the almost permanently stormy north shore. *Maui*'s west coast, especially Kaanapali, is every bit as good as Waikiki. On the south coast, try Seven Pools. *Molokai* is really not for swimming, except on the west coast

Sailing out past Diamond Head just as the storm hits Punchbowl.

with its private access roads. *Lanai*'s Hulopoe Beach is usually good and safe. On *Kauai*, your best bets are Poipu, Anini and Wailua. There is freshwater swimming at Hanakoa and Wailua Falls.

If you want to go **snorkeling** and **scuba-diving,** consult the local dive shops for renting equipment, taking lessons and obtaining up-to-date information about current conditions. On *Oahu*, diving is good off Manana (Rabbit) Island and at Hanauma Bay, the Waianae Coast beaches and, summer only, the North Shore beaches. *Hawaii* snorkeling is best in the coves from Kawaihae to Puako, Keauhou Beach and Spencer Beach. *Maui* snorkelers go around the rocks at Kapalua, Kamaole, Napili and Wailea. On *Molokai*, expert swimmers skin-dive in Halawa Bay. *Lanai* snorkelers love Hulopoe. *Kauai* has good snorkeling at Poipu, Anini and Haena.

Beachcombing is, for the non-swimmer, the best way to get your feet wet. You won't find much in the way of shipwreck flotsam but there are still a few lovely sea shells. If you venture out into the tidepools or over the reef at low tide to inspect the marine life, remember two pointers: 1) wear thicksoled "thongs" or tennis shoes;

Beach Beaux
One of the more intriguing phenomena to have arisen from Hawaii's enduring love affair with the sea is the beachboy. This bronzed, swaggering expert at swimming, surfing, snorkeling, scuba-diving and any other sibilant sea-sport has established himself as a boon to the lonelyhearts, but also as a very useful instructor. In order to ply his talents, he has a license from the Hawaii State Department of Transportation. The ones who offer expertise in sailing must also be licensed by the U.S. Coast Guard. Their extracurricular activities, absolutely essential for completing their image, are not licensed.

2) don't disturb the marine life you're looking at. If you pick up a rock to see what's underneath, try to put it carefully back the way you found it. Think of it as the sea-creatures' furniture and of yourself as a privileged guest.

Sailing on catamarans and trimarans is available at most resort centers. You might also try **canoeing.** Boats can be hired and instruction is available for novices, the best being out of Lahaina, *Maui,* and Kailua on the *Big Island.*

In addition to ubiquitous line-fishing and surfcasting, **deep-sea fishing** is a delight on **93** most of the Islands, with marlin, tuna, *mahimahi* and barracuda being the main targets. From *Oahu* you can charter a boat at the Kewalo Marine Basin in Honolulu. These sail off Koko Head to the Penguin Banks off *Molokai* or off the Waianae Coast. For the latter, you can also charter at Pokai Bay and at Haleiwa for the North Shore. On *Maui*, the charters are at Lahaina and Maalaea Bay. Go spear-fishing for octopus at Hana. *Hawaii* offers its charters out of Kailua. Try night-trolling (bottom-fishing) at Isaac Hale Beach Park. There is good freshwater fishing for mullet at the Waiakea Pond in the Wailoa River State Park at Hilo. *Kauai* is better for surfcasting and spear-fishing, especially on the reefs off Poipu and around Hanalei.

Sports on Land

Hunting is, of course, seasonal—November 1 to mid-January for birds, with animal seasons to be checked with the local offices of the Division of Fish and Game. *Oahu* has wild pig, pheasant, partridge and dove. *Hawaii* has bow-and-arrow hunting for wild sheep and pig, in addition to conventional hunting for wild goat, boar and the game birds. *Maui* offers deer, boar, quail, pheasant and dove. There's goat on Haleakala. *Molokai* and *Lanai* both have deer, goat and mouflon sheep. *Kauai* has a lot of wild pig in the forests and goat in the Waimea Canyon.

For those who want to taste the joys of Hawaii without succumbing to the easier pleasures of civilized hotels, resort-complexes and condominiums, the **hiking** and **camping** are superb. With the added bonus of there being no snakes, no poisonous insects and no poison ivy. The

Division of Forestry, State Department of Land and Natural Resources, will give you all the information you need on trails and permits (free). *Kauai* and *Maui* stand out as the best islands for getting off the beaten track. You'll need a sleeping bag if you want to do some camping at higher altitudes; otherwise a light blanket and inflatable mattress suffice. Take drinking water with you.

Riding—horses on *Maui*, *Kauai* and the *Big Island*, mules on *Molokai*—takes on a new dimension in Hawaii. One of the most exciting excursions any horse-man or -woman can make is into Maui's Haleakala Crater (see p. 63), where three cabins each provide twelve beds for a rest between the eerie delight of a volcano by moon- and starlight and a sunrise trot across the caldera.

There are dozens of good trails on Maui's grassy Hana coast—a good way to get closer to nature.

held at Waialae Golf and Country Club, Honolulu, in January.

Spectator sports, mostly centered on *Oahu*, include the usual (but not very high-level) **baseball** and **football,** the best being the Hula Bowl all-star game in January. The **basketball** is good college-level. Japanese **Sumo wrestling** can be seen in Honolulu, where there is even a **cricket** club immaculate enough to satisfy the most fastidious Englishman. International **surfing championships** are held on Oahu in November and December.

But perhaps the most popular sport in Hawaii—and one not likely to die out as a mere fad—is **jogging.** All over the islands, fat, thin, long and short, everyone and his grandmother pants along the beaches and parks, even—heaven knows why—through the dense traffic of downtown Honolulu. If you need an incentive or objective to motivate your jogging, the only sport that manages to be both exhilarating and boring, start before sunrise around the Haleakala Crater on *Maui*, make the sunset run through Waimea Bay Beach Park on *Oahu*—or phone for the next eruption at Kilauea on the *Big Island* and beat the lava flow down to the beach.

The **golf** and **tennis** possibilities are endless, the best resort facilities being at *Maui*'s Kaanapali, *Hawaii*'s Mauna Kea and *Oahu*'s Makaha. There's also good public tennis at *Oahu*'s Ala Moana, *Kauai*'s Coco Palms and *Hawaii*'s Kailua-Kona. The international Hawaii Open Golf Tournament is

Shopping

Shopping Hours

In Waikiki, one or two coffee shops and stores open 24 hours, but shopping hours of department stores and other shops are usually 9:30 a.m. to 9 p.m. Outer Island shops close much earlier than those in Honolulu.

Shopping Tips

1) Don't buy anything you can't carry away from Hawaii yourself; trying to have the store ship it for you is a very risky business; 2) don't always

After a strenuous hike, what about shelling out for some souvenirs?

expect something to look as beautiful back home as it does in Hawaii—those exotic tropical colors can be very disquieting away from their exotic tropical context; 3) Hawaii is a good place to buy things strictly for use on the spot. The Hawaiian shirts and dresses, Japanese *zori* thong-sandals and beach mats are best bought very cheap so that you won't feel sad when they fall apart at the end of your vacation and can't be taken home.

Leis

Leis, the famous tokens of welcome and farewell, were worn around the neck in ancient Hawaii as a regular form of personal adornment, with the most splendid coming out on ceremonial occasions. Nowadays they are made of orchids, carnations, plumeria, kika, ginger and jasmine blossoms, but were originally of leaves, ferns, shells, fruit, beads and bright-colored bird-feathers. The time-honored superstition is that when you leave Hawaii by boat, you toss the *lei* on the water and if it floats back to shore, you will come back again some day. If it sinks or follows you out to sea, you're not going to see Hawaii ever again. Which is why people prefer jumbo jets.

Best Buys

If, however, you do develop a passion for the florid-patterned **clothes**—and the long loose fit does make eminently good sense in hot humid climates—you can have them made to measure. Go for the fast-colored 100 percent cottons and silks that will hold up more than one season.

Some masks may look more Viking than Polynesian, but a hat's a hat.

The happy-go-lucky atmosphere has somehow made the Hawaii tee-shirt motifs more amusing than elsewhere, if funny tee-shirts are your taste.

When Hawaiian flowers are not decorating shirts and *muumuu* dresses, they turn up as candles and candy. Be careful. Some of these are almost identical in size and shape, and the labels deceptively similar. Your kid may end up biting off a lump of orchid-scented wax.

You can also, of course, buy

the **flowers** as flowers—most often as *lei*. The most popular are plumeria or frangipani, orchids, anthuriums and gardenias, best if boxed on your last day for the trip home. But some flowers (e.g. gardenias) are not permitted to be imported into California (see p. 117).

Artifacts

Wood-carving and ceramics are not among Hawaii's most delicate craftwork, although you can get *tikis* (gods) of local woods or of lava. You'll have better luck with the coral **jewelry** on Maui. There are some pretty *lauhala* tree and coconut fiber products—mats, hats, purses and sandals woven from leaves of the pandanus tree—one of the few remaining authentic Hawaiian handicrafts. Ukuleles are most often imported from Japan and Taiwan, but that is no reason not to buy one: you're more likely to find them in Hawaii than anywhere else (some, though, are

made of local *koa* wood). And if you're taking up surfing seriously and have somewhere to do it back home, then Hawaii does have the best **surfboards**, custom-made or mass-produced.

If you haven't had enough **pineapples** already, you can take home boxes of them, the best bargains being right on the plantations. Some local brandy (called *Okolehao*) is produced with a distinctive touch of *ti*-plant flavor. As for other exotic fruits, there are jellies and jams, chutneys and syrups, of guava, papaya, poha, and mango. Not forgetting the famed macadamia nut.

One of the most amusing gifts is a smooth-husked **coconut,** on which you just write the address and stick a stamp. Mail it and the Hawaiian branch of the U.S. Post Office promises delivery.

Nightlife

On the island of Oahu, in Honolulu and Waikiki, the entertainment very much resembles Las Vegas without the casinos (gambling is illegal in Hawaii)—nightclubs with singers, comedians and often lavish floorshows. Elsewhere the scene is strictly disco.

The floorshows will often feature *hula* dancing, some of it chaste enough to satisfy the most puritanical missionaries, but also occasionally topless and even bottomless, in a style resembling the original dances of the ancient Hawaiians only in the amount of clothing worn.

Outside the nightclubs and

That woven straw, made today into bags or tablemats, served as beds for the islanders of yesterday. **101**

dance performed unsmilingly before a gathering of royalty and commoners. It was accompanied by a gourd-drum for the rhythm and a chant known as the *hula hoopaa*. After the formal performance everybody joined in and the atmosphere relaxed. Another *hula* was the *kui* danced by the warriors to alleviate battle fatigue.

The dancers used to emphasize the erotic elements of the *hula* when performing aboard ship for European and American sailors. Gradually the music was brightened with the introduction of the Portuguese *machada* guitar, which became the ukulele, a Hawaiian word meaning "jumping insect" or flea. The dancers added steps learned from the Europeans.

When King Kalakaua officially revived *hula* dancing for his 1882 coronation, after the long missionary ban, the local American-owned *Hawaiian Gazette* condemned it as a "monstrous incarnation of brutishness, the benighted phallic worship, representative of all that is animal and gross". The printer of the coronation *hula* dance program—with its songs and dances in honor of various parts of the body—was fined for producing an obscene publication.

discos, Hawaii's best evening show is its sunset, moon and stars, for which private enterprise has laid on cruises in motor yachts and catamarans, complete with dinner and music. The best of these are available from Waikiki, Kailua and Lahaina.

The Hula

The original *hula* was a sacred ritual performed by a special class of men and women to praise their chiefs, honor the gods or promote fecundity. The dancers were highly specialized and trained in a *hula* school known as the *halau*. Typically, the *hula olapa* was a

Dining

Like so many things on Hawaii, wining and dining are not to be taken too seriously. The food and drink often have more fun than finesse in them. There are, however, some very good, award-winning restaurants on the islands, particularly in Honolulu.

Meal Times

Hawaii residents eat early and most restaurants do not serve past 10 p.m. Cocktail lounges stay open until 1 a.m. to 4 a.m., depending on their type of license.

Specialties

There *are* some Hawaiian delicacies but they're difficult to run down. The best of them used to form the centerpiece of the *luau*, the traditional Hawaiian banquet. The *luau* is now a feature of most resort hotels' guest-entertainment, though not always with specifically Hawaiian cuisine. *Lomi lomi* is a dish of salmon that has been hand-massaged to break down the tissue and remove the salt. The salmon is mixed in chunks with tomatoes and onion. Nobody roasts dog any more, but you will find *kalua pig*. A whole pig is gutted and then packed with salt and placed in the middle of

the *imu*, an oven of burning-hot rocks, and baked slowly for hours.

Other meat dishes and fish such as *mahimahi* (dolphin fish, an island delicacy not the dolphin mammal), *tuna*, *opakapaka* (pink snapper), *humuhumunukunukuapuaa* (try that one for pronunciation) are prepared

A botanical paradise—exotic blooms offer a kaleidoscope of colour in the most unexpected places.

Hawaiian-style in a papillote of *ti*-palm leaves and steamed among the baking rocks of the *imu*.

The universal accompanying vegetable to the fish and meat for Polynesian Hawaiians and occasionally served as an alternative to mashed potatoes is *poi*. This is the root of the *taro* plant,

peeled, cooked and mashed into a paste, then fermented —an acquired taste that few *malihini* acquire. The *taro* bulb can also be eaten, chopped and steamed in *ti*-leaves.

Pineapple is served with practically everything—it's even employed in a spaghetti sauce—and when it's not, there's always coconut.

"Ethnic" Cuisines

When "Polynesian touches" are resisted, the Islands' cuisine is much that of its settlers—traditional American, of course, but also very good Japanese and Chinese. The Hawaiians have extended Japanese *teriyaki* marinades of fish and beef to their ultimate Americanization—"teriburgers". You'll find Chinese *dim sum* dumplings all over Honolulu at small sidewalk stands as well as part of the menu in Chinese restaurants. The Portuguese contributions are their hot sausage, the *malasada* doughnuts and *pão doce* sweetbread.

The French imitations are for the most part pretentious and expensive and the Italians merely expensive. There are a couple of Irish restaurants in Honolulu and Waikiki where the whiskey in the coffee is excellent and well worth trying—without the coffee. **105**

Drinks

As for local brews, you may be lucky enough to come across the hooch known as *okolehao* or simply *oke,* distilled from *ti*-palm roots. Properly aged, it's a potent brandy that some Kauai residents claim is at the true etymological origin of the word "O.K.". There's a Californian gentleman on Maui manufacturing a white pineapple wine available in a few shops under the name of *Maui blanc.* He also has brought out a sparkling wine (from grapes this time) from Hawaii's only vineyard, on a ranch at Ulupalakua.

Then there are the rum-based drinks which are not indigenous, but abound in local names once they've crossed their powerful white liquors with crushed pineapples, bananas, papaya and any other sweet tropical fruit. If you're driving within three months of your cocktail, drink one or two but never more of such concoctions as "Diamond Head Dynamite", the "Kilauea Killer" and "Haleakala Hellfire". Perhaps the most innocent-sounding—but most lethal—is the "Molokai Cocktail", more appropriately named for Molotov.

Cocktails of fruits or flowers, but always with a fiery dose of rum.

BERLITZ-INFO

How to Get There

From North America

BY AIR: There are direct scheduled flights every day from approximately two dozen major metropolitan areas, with the best service from Los Angeles, San Francisco and Seattle/Tacoma (a 5- to 5¹/₂-hour trip). Daily connecting flights leave to Honolulu from cities in almost every

state of the U.S., as well as San Juan in Puerto Rico. From Canada more than a dozen cities are linked via daily flights to Honolulu.

Charter Flights and Package Tours: There are numerous GIT (Group Inclusive Tour) programs currently available from 8 to 15 days in length, with visits scheduled to one or all six of the Hawaiian Islands. Tour features include air transportation, hotel accommodations, some or all meals, transfers, sightseeing and flights between the islands. A special feature on some tours is the use of a car for a day or longer. For those who want to stop on the mainland as part of the trip, stop-overs are offered in Los Angeles, San Francisco, Las Vegas, Portland or Seattle. In addition, the Hawaiian Islands are featured as four-day "extensions" on fifteen-day or longer GITs to the Orient.

BY SEA: If time isn't a major factor you can take a cruise from California to Honolulu aboard one of the regular lines based in New York or San Francisco. Cruising time from California to Hawaii is five days. Many of the trips include stops in other Pacific destinations such as Tahiti or even Australia and New Zealand. There are combination air-sea packages between the West Coast and Hawaii which take about 12 days—you fly either to or from the islands and take a cruise in the other direction.

From Great Britain

BY AIR: Daily flights leave Heathrow for US gateway cities such as New York, Washington, Miami, San Francisco and Los Angeles, with same-day connections for Honolulu.

Charter Flights and Package Tours can also be arranged by your travel agent. Advanced Booking Charters (ABC) are a little cheaper than APEX but are regarded as secondary in importance to scheduled flights and leave from Gatwick.

Within the US there are special concessions available to foreign tourists which should be booked before departure. An Airpass allows you 30 days unlimited travel on the mainland, and similar tickets are available for trains and motor coaches. There's a special combination air fare, the VUSA (Visit USA), which permits discounts on both parts of your journey—to the USA and within it—if booked well enough in advance. Savings can be up to 40% on domestic flights. Your travel agent will be able to find the most economical flight out to Hawaii for you whether you decide to fly straight to the West Coast or to the East Coast and travel across independently.

For visitors wishing to discover the islands, the Visit Hawaii excursion offers 30 days unlimited travel between the islands. The ticket must be purchased abroad. See also AIR TOURS, p. 112.

Package holidays to Hawaii are widely available. Their prices are usually based on APEX fares, and bookings can be made later at Excursion rates. With an APEX-based package you can spend the extra time your fare allows (APEX limits of stay are 7–60 days) traveling or sightseeing independently.

When to Go

Since the Islands are in the tropics, temperatures remain fairly stable year round; in lowlands, such as at Waikiki, the temperatures range from an average low of 65°F to an average high of 80° in winter and slightly warmer in summer. Trade winds from the east and northeast keep the air balmy most of the year. In summer the *kona*, a leeward wind, may bring sticky weather; in winter it may mean gales and storms. Winter trade winds bring frequent rain to many areas, but in spring and summer showers are few.

The following chart will give you an idea of the average monthly temperatures in Honolulu:

	J	F	M	A	M	J	J	A	S	O	N	D
°F	72	72	73	75	77	79	85	85	85	79	77	74
°C	22	22	23	24	25	26	29	29	29	26	25	23
Inches of rain	4.4	2.5	3.2	1.4	1	.3	.6	.8	.7	1.5	3	3.7

Planning Your Budget

To give you an idea of what to expect in Hawaii, here's a list of some average prices. They must be regarded as approximate, however, as inflation creeps relentlessly up. Island prices tend to be higher than those on the Mainland.

Airport transfer. Public bus to Waikiki hotels 60¢, limousine $6, taxi $20.

Air tours. All-island airtour $255, helicopter tour Na Pali Coast (Kauai) $125–150 per person.

Baby-sitters. $6.50 an hour, 50¢ per hour for each additional child; generally minimum four hours, $2 for transportation.

Bicycle, motorcycle and moped rental. Bicycle $10 to 20 a day, motorcycle $30 to 60 a day, moped from $15 to 25 a day.

Car rental. Varies widely: $25 to 50 a day with unlimited mileage. Flydrive plans to the Outer Islands via various islands can give you a special deal the first day the car is rented.

Cigarettes. From $2.40 a pack.

Cinema. From $5.50.

Guides. By bus $15 to 20, by van $20 to 40, by limousine $15 to 30.

Hairdressers. *Man's* haircut $10 and up. *Woman's* haircut $20 to 50, shampoo and set $25–35, shampoo and blow-dry $15 to 25, color rinse/dye $50–100.

Hotels (double room with bath). Lower-price category $40 to 75, medium priced $75 to 150, higher priced $150 to 400 ($15 to 25 surcharges per night from Dec. 20 to April in some hotels).

Meals and drinks. Breakfast $7.50 to 15, lunch (in fairly good establishment) $10 to 20, dinner $15 to 50, coffee $1 to 1.50, beer $2 to 4, wine (bottle) $10 and up, cocktail $3.50 and up.

Nightclubs/Discotheques. Cover charge $5 to 10 with two-drink minimum.

Shopping. 6- and 8-packs of pineapples $15 to 20, Hawaiian charms from $25, *hula* skirts from $15, *muumuus* (long) from $45, *aloha* shirts from $25.

Sightseeing. Boats $15 to 40, museums $10 (children generally half price).

Taxis. Meters start at $1.50, plus $1.50 for each additional mile.

An A–Z Summary of Practical Information and Facts

A star (★) following an entry indicates that relevant prices are to be found on page 110.

Some information contained in this blueprint will already be familiar to U.S. residents, but has been included to be of help to visitors from overseas.

AIRPORTS★. Honolulu International Airport, on the Island of Oahu, is one of the busiest in the U.S.; not only is the number of flights growing rapidly, but its facilities are also being expanded. The present complex, begun in the early 1960's, has been developed for jumbo jet traffic. There are three main concourses in the overseas terminal, with frequent shuttle bus service to departure gates and baggage claim areas.

The airport boasts a bank, post office, restaurants, bar, barbershop, shower facilities, *lei* (flower garland) stands, shops, a currency exchange office (open till 3:30 a.m.) and a duty-free shop. Three gardens—one Hawaiian, one Chinese and one Japanese—grace the central area of the airport.

A traveler's assistance office takes care of people in trouble, while State Department of Transportation hostesses in *muumuu* dresses and straw hats will answer any questions.

City buses leave every 10 minutes from the airport's second level for the 45- to 60-minute ride to Waikiki hotels. (No baggage is allowed on city buses.) The limousine (motor coach) service (two bags allowed free with an additional charge for each extra piece) takes about 25 minutes.

Shuttle buses from the overseas terminal to the interisland and commuter terminals run regularly all day. There is good and frequent air service to Hawaii's Outer Islands by the all-jet interisland airlines as well as smaller commuter air taxi firms. The interisland terminal has a coffee shop and bar.

Some direct flights from the U.S. mainland fly to Kona on Hawaii Island, to Kahului on Maui and to Lihue on Kauai. Smaller Outer Island airports are served only by the interisland airlines. Regular scheduled interisland flights are frequent and take an average of 30 minutes or so. From Outer Island airports there is no public transportation into the center of town, but transfers to tour buses can be made without problems.

A

A **AIR TOURS***. The chances are you'll go to Honolulu/Waikiki first and longest, but it's a pity to stay there the whole time when there are such exciting and varied possibilities on other islands.

If time is limited, one carrier from Honolulu does a day tour of all eight islands showing from the air some of the most spectacular sights (that can't anyhow be seen from the ground) and one or two of the top land sights as well. There are more leisurely tours, also, taking up to a week, and covering the three major islands.

Helicopter flights give a new perspective on volcanoes, craters, waterfalls and inaccessible coasts and canyons, and can be taken from most islands; somewhat expensive, they offer a unique experience that is well worth trying.

B **BICYCLE, MOTORCYCLE and MOPED RENTAL***. Several agencies in Waikiki (listed in the Yellow Pages of the telephone directory) rent bicycles, motorcycles and mopeds. Alternatively your hotel will probably recommend companies or even have bicycles for rent. Mopeds have now become quite popular on the Outer Islands as well.

C **CAMPING.** Visitors may camp in various public beach parks on Oahu and the Neighbor Islands, but only in self-contained campers, as there's no water hookup, electricity or toilet facilities in these parks. Free permits may be obtained from the Parks and Recreation Department in the Honolulu Municipal Building at King and Alapai Streets and in the county buildings on the Outer Islands. Mobile homes or campers that can be hired from local agencies on the bigger islands provide very complete camping and living arrangements. It's best to avoid beaches on the western shore of Oahu as there has been a rather high number of burglaries from rented cars and trailers (caravans).

For information on camping in Haleakala Crater, write to the Superintendent, Haleakala National Park:

Box 369 Makawao, Maui HI 96768 (tel. 572-9306).
You can ring 572-9177 for recorded information on camping.

For information on camping in state parks on Maui, write to the Division of State Parks, Hawaii Department of Land and Natural Resources:

State Building, Wailuku, Maui HI 96793 (tel. 243-5354).

CAR RENTAL*. See also DRIVING. Car rental companies are highly
competitive in Hawaii, with about 30 agencies in Honolulu and any-

where from 5 to 10 on the Outer Islands. Rates and requirements vary widely, so check carefully as to what you are agreeing to before signing, and shop around if you have time. You can rent everything from four-wheel-drive vehicles and foreign subcompacts to luxury American cars.

To rent a car, American citizens must have a valid driver's license, while foreigners need an International Driving License. Depending on the company, the minimum age is from 21 to 25 and some agencies set a maximum age of 70. Large deposits are required unless you have a major credit card. Beware of drop-off charges: in Honolulu, for example, if you rent a car in Waikiki and leave it at the airport, you may have to pay an additional charge. And on the Island of Hawaii, many visitors pick up a car in Hilo and leave it in Kona, costing an additional $10.

CHILDREN*. There is a lot to do in Honolulu for the young and the young at heart.

Honolulu Zoo at the Diamond Head end of Waikiki is open daily from 8:30 a.m. to 4 p.m. and is free for children 12 and under accompanied by an adult. The zoo has petting pens, a barn and picnic grounds. The state-owned Waikiki Aquarium, also at the Diamond Head end of Waikiki, is free for children under 16.

And then there is always the beach, of course. Kuhio Beach in Waikiki and Ala Moana Beach are both safe for children—who should nevertheless always be supervised by an adult able to swim. There are lifeguards at these beaches.

The larger hotels have planned activities for children and provide babysitting services—or can at least put you in touch with a reputable agency.

If your child gets lost, call the Honolulu Police Department or the county police department on the Outer Islands (see POLICE).

CIGARETTES, CIGARS, TOBACCO*. Cigarettes are more expensive when bought from a vending machine and cheaper when purchased by the carton in drugstores, sundry stores and grocery stores.

Tobacco, American and imported, is also available in drugstores and tobacco shops.

CLOTHING. Hawaii is casual and visitors soon find themselves dressing accordingly. Year-round you'll need nothing heavier than summer clothing, although in winter a wrap or sweater will come in handy at night. So, essentially, travel light.

Some better restaurants require men to wear a coat and tie, so check when making reservations.

Women will probably want to purchase a colorful *muumuu* (dress) or two (they come in all shapes and sizes, and colors, too), and men some bright *aloha* shirts. Hats are advisable, and there's a broad choice of fibers and fabrics on the spot.

You may see signs requesting that shoes be worn (this shows how casual things are!) and in this instance sandals will generally do. Equally, most hotels don't appreciate guests walking through lobbies in bathing suits.

From November to March, Hawaii is generally rainy, and while a raincoat may be too heavy for muggy days, an umbrella will come in handy—though Hawaiians breeze through without! If your vacation includes trips to cool summits (e.g. Mauna Kea on Big Island or Haleakala on Maui), don't forget something warm.

COMMUNICATIONS. The U.S. Postal Service deals exclusively with mail. Hotels generally sell stamps. Vending machines also have stamps, but you pay more than the face value of the stamps you receive.

Post office hours: 8 a.m. to 4 p.m. Mondays through Fridays and 8 a.m. to noon on Saturdays.

Mail: If you don't know ahead of time where you will be staying, you may have mail addressed to you General Delivery (Poste Restante) at Honolulu HI 96802 (the post office at Honolulu International Airport). Should you be one of the Outer Islands, have mail addressed General Delivery to the town you are staying in.

If you do know what hotel you will be staying at, mail addressed to you should have the date of your arrival in the lower left-hand corner of the envelope.

There is a post office in Waikiki at 330 Saratoga Road.

The American Express Office: 2222 Kalakaua Avenue, Suite 803, Honolulu HI 96815.

Take your driver's license or passport with you to claim mail.

Telegrams: Telegraph companies in the U.S. are privately owned. For telegraph services see listings in the Yellow Pages. Night letters may be sent to the U.S. Mainland by calling either the telephone company or one of the telegraph companies.

Telephone: There's no extra charge for calls within the same island. It is cheaper to make a call from a pay phone as hotels generally charge more.

However, if you want to make a long-distance call, it's simpler to do so from your hotel room. U.S. visitors will find phoning long-distance the same as on the Mainland, though the rates are a little higher.

For international calls, dial 011, then the country code, the area code and the local telephone number. Country and city routing codes are listed in the telephone directory. If the code you want is not listed, dial 1-555-1313 for assistance. To obtain a telephone number abroad, dial 0.

COMPLAINTS. If you have problems with a hotel, restaurant or shop, try speaking to the manager first. If that doesn't work, the Hawaii Visitors Bureau has an efficient Visitor Satisfaction Department at 2270 Kalakaua Avenue, Honolulu; tel. 923-1811.

You can also turn to the State of Hawaii Office of Consumer Protection: 828 Fort Street Mall, Honolulu; tel. 587-3222.

CONSULATES. Australia is the only English-speaking country to have a full-fledged consulate in Hawaii, serving foreign English speakers:

Penthouse, 1000 Bishop Street, Honolulu HI 96813; tel. 524-5050. Hours: 8 a.m. to 4 p.m. Mondays through Fridays.

CRIME and THEFT. You may be feeling relaxed on vacation, but don't relax too much. Put valuables in your hotel safe and do not leave any personal effects of value (including your room key) on the beach while you swim. Equally, don't leave anything in your car that would attract thieves; cars, even locked ones, are easy targets in popular, and populous, sightseeing areas. Despite occasional press reports of hostility and even violence, Hawaii remains essentially a safe place, providing common-sense rules of behavior are applied.

DRIVING IN HAWAII. Driving is a good way to see the islands—on some islands virtually the only way. In parts of the islands it can be difficult, not to say hair-raising, e.g. Maui.

Be sure to follow traffic signs, as there can be confusing traffic patterns, particularly in Honolulu. Drivers are generally polite and you'll hear little horn-honking—it simply isn't done except in dire circum-

D stances. Speed limits on paved streets are generally 25 or 35 m. p. h., and are posted. Expressway speeds are from 40 to 55 m. p. h. Such limits are strictly enforced.

You'll find it less hectic if you avoid rush hours—from 6: 30 to 8: 30 a.m. and 3: 30 to 5: 30 p. m. when commuters are on the move. At some intersections left turns are not permitted during these hours (signs are posted). You may turn right at red lights unless a sign indicates otherwise.

The possession of any liquor in a car means a large fine and the probability of a year in jail. Driving under the influence of alcohol is a criminal offense, and is punished severely.

Parking: The larger hotels have parking—for a fee. Finding a parking place on the street can be difficult and many areas have tow-away zones during rush hours. Again, they are well marked.

Parking in downtown Honolulu is difficult; private lots are expensive and municipal lots fill up early in the day.

Gasoline and Oil: Gas is available in premium, regular and unleaded. Later model American cars take only unleaded gasoline, which is more expensive than regular. If your car breaks down, call the rental agency.

E **ELECTRIC CURRENT.** Hawaii is on the standard U.S. 110-volt 60-cycle current, and plugs have the regular two flat prongs. Visitors from abroad will need an adaptor for their electric razors and other appliances, best purchased before leaving home.

EMERGENCIES. On Oahu, Maui and Kauai you can reach the police, fire department and ambulance by dialing 911. On Hawaii island, call 961-6022 for ambulance or fire department. Numbers for police vary according to the area. It's best to dial 0 and an operator will help you. In hotels, you should call the hotel security department.

Other handy Oahu numbers:
Coast Guard Rescue: tel. 1-800-552-6458
Dentist: tel. 536-2135
Doctor: tel. 536-6988
Hawaii Poison Center: tel. 941-4411
Sex Abuse Treatment Center: tel. 524-7273
Suicide and Crisis Center: tel. 521-4555
Waikiki Life Guard: tel: 922-3888

Hotels either have doctors on the premises or on call.

ENTRY FORMALITIES and CUSTOMS CONTROLS. Canadians need only evidence of their nationality to enter Hawaii. Other foreign visitors need a valid passport and a visitor's visa, which can be obtained at any U.S. consulate or embassy. They also have to fill out customs declaration forms before arriving (usually distributed in the aircraft during the flight).

The following chart shows what main duty-free items you may take into the U.S. and, when returning home, into your own country:

Into:	Cigarettes	Cigars	Tobacco	Spirits	Wine
U.S.A.	200 or	50 or	1,350 g.	1 l. or	1 l.
Australia	200 or	250 g. or	250 g.	1 l. or	1 l.
Canada	200 and	50 and	900 g.	1.1 l. or	1.1 l.
Eire	200 or	50 or	250 g.	1 l. and	2 l.
N. Zealand	200 or	50 or	250 g.	1.1 l. and	4.5 l.
S. Africa	400 and	50 and	250 g.	1 l. and	2 l.
U.K.	200 or	50 or	250 g.	1 l. and	2 l.

A non-resident may bring in duty-free up to $100 in gifts if he stays 72 hours or more and has not claimed this exemption within the preceding six months.

Plants and foodstuffs are subject to strict control; Mainland Americans and visitors from abroad may not bring in certain fruits, vegetables or meat. Nor may they, on the way back to the U.S. Mainland, take out the following items: berries of any kind, including coffee berries; cactus plants or parts; cotton and cotton bolls; fresh flowers of gardenia, jade vine, mauna loa, and rose; fruit (except coconuts and pineapples); live insects and snails; plants in soil; rose plants or parts; fresh seed pods; soil; sugarcane.

Arriving and departing passengers must report any money or checks exceeding a total of $10,000.

Foreign visitors arriving at Honolulu Airport in the morning should be prepared for long waits at customs; flights tend to arrive at the same time and up to two hours can be spent hanging around (coming from the U.S. Mainland, however, no visitors have to go through customs on arrival in Honolulu).

G **GUIDES*.** There is a variety of organized tours around Oahu and the Neighbor Islands and many companies will tailor tours to the interests and requirements of clients. The tour companies are regulated by the State Public Utilities Commission and rates are standard. Hotels have tour desks and many travel agents have offices in Waikiki.

There are dozens of walking tours of downtown Honolulu. The staff of the Mission Houses Museum organizes walks of historic Honolulu. Equally, there are 45-minute tours through Iolani Palace, the only royal palace in the U.S. (reservations are required and there is heavy demand). The *Falls of Clyde*, launched by Scotland's Falls Lines just over 100 years ago, is the last full-rigged, four-masted sailing vessel remaining in Hawaii (Pier 7 in Hololulu Harbor). The Chinese Chamber of Commerce has a 3-hour tour of Chinatown, and Foster Botanical Gardens, an oasis in downtown Honolulu, offers free tours. For further details, see SIGHTSEEING HOURS.

H **HAIRDRESSERS*.** Prices vary widely so best get quotes by calling the establishments. There is no service charge included in the cost and therefore it's customary to tip unless the hairdresser is the owner. Most large hotels have their own salons, but you can generally find lower prices at smaller shops.

HOTELS and ACCOMMODATIONS*. There is a wide range of hotels in Hawaii, one for every taste and budget. The vast majority are European Plan, though a select few are Modified American Plan. Advance booking is a must from December 20 to Easter. July and August are also busy months and reservations are necessary, but it's *always* wise to make advance reservations in Hawaii, in case you arrive at a time when some large convention is being held.

The Hawaii Visitors Bureau publishes an annual guide to its member hotels, listing rates and amenities, but in no way attempts to categorize the hotels. Condominiums and homes are available for rent for longer periods, generally through agencies. In the winter months, these, too, are booked well in advance.

Hotels on the beach generally charge higher rates, with ocean-front rooms more expensive than those facing the mountains.

L **LANGUAGE.** You're highly unlikely to hear Hawaiian spoken on the street, except words and phrases mixed into Pidgin English—which is spoken by everyone who grew up in the islands—the further away from Oahu the more "outlandish". It's easy to pick up and very colorful.

But the Hawaiian language still exists. It's a dialect of the Polynesian tongue, other variations of which are spoken by the Samoans, Tahitians, Marquesans and New Zealand Maoris. One or two clues about the language to help you pronounce Hawaiian street and place names:

The Hawaiian alphabet consists of 12 letters; the vowels are the same as those in English (Y doesn't exist, however). The consonants are restricted to H, K, L, M, N, P and W.

The vowels are pronounced as follows:

A as in r*a*ther, E like in f*ei*gn, I (long "ee" sound) as in cr*ee*p, O as in *o*cean and U (long again, an "oo" sound) as in s*ou*p.

The consonants generally are pronounced as in English.

All you have to do now is remember four invariable rules: Every word must end in a vowel; every consonant has to be followed by one vowel at least; each syllable must end in a vowel; divide into syllables to be able to pronounce easily, e.g. Wa-i-ma-na-lo.

For practical purposes, here are a few of the most common expressions you're likely to hear:

aloha	hello, goodbye, love	**mahalo**	thank you
hale	house	**ono**	delicious
kane	man	**pali**	cliffs
kaukau	food	**pau**	finished
keiki	child	**puka**	hole
kokua	help	**wahine**	woman
luau	feast	**wikiwiki**	fast, quick

LAUNDRY and DRY-CLEANING. If your hotel doesn't look after laundry or dry-cleaning and is without a self-service laundry, there are several commercial laundries and dry-cleaners in Waikiki. Same-day service is generally quite a bit more expensive than the regular charge.

LOST and FOUND. If loss or suspected theft occur in your hotel, check first at the reception desk. They may suggest you report the incident to the police. If you trace your steps to the shops or restaurants you visited, you will probably find the item has been turned in. If you've lost your passport, check with your consulate (if there is one in Honolulu) or, again, the police headquarters.

MAPS. Maps are given away at car rental agencies, hotels, tour desks and the Hawaii Visitors Bureau. Free tourist publications are also avail-

M able either in your hotel or from street stands. While such maps are perfectly adequate for getting around, they are not very detailed. More precise maps can be purchased from book shops; an excellent series, one for each island, is produced by Hawaiian Service Inc., P.O. Box 2835, Honolulu, HI 96803.

MEDICAL CARE. Foreigners should note that the U.S. doesn't provide free medical services, and medical treatment is expensive. Arrangements should therefore be made in advance for temporary health insurance (through a travel agent or an insurance company); alternatively, ask at the local Social Security office for precise information on coverage during your trip to the U.S.

If you arrive in Hawaii after flying through several time zones, take it easy the first couple of days. Doctors recommend visitors to eat lightly initially, and to get plenty of rest. Jet lag fatigue may only set in on the second day.

Be careful of the tropical sun. Hawaii is much closer to the sun's rays than visitors from northern climates may be aware of. Fair-skinned visitors find it takes a mere few minutes to turn red. The sun's rays are doubly lethal on the beach because of glare from water and sand. Strong sunglasses are a good investment as is a suntan lotion—but *with* a sunscreen. Try to do your sunning in small doses the first few days and stay out of direct sunlight between 11 a.m. and 2 p.m. when the ultraviolet rays are at their most intense.

Many of Hawaii's exotic drinks are rum-based and pack a more powerful punch than is apparent at first sip. Two are plenty.

Visitors from Great Britain will find that a certain number of drugs they are used to buying over the counter at home can only be purchased by prescription in the U.S. There's no shortage of drugstores and pharmacies, many of them in Waikiki open late at night.

Contact the hotel or the police for a list of doctors.

MEETING PEOPLE. You will meet people easily anywhere—from lively nightspots to the beach. You will find Hawaii residents very friendly and outgoing—part of their famed *aloha* spirit—and don't be surprised to be included in an impromptu party or game of volleyball on the beach. For the younger set, discos abound in Waikiki. Most bars and lounges have half-price "happy hours" in the late afternoon, a popular place for friends (and soon-to-be friends) to gather.

There are holidays and festivals year-long, with great opportunities to sample the local culture and meet Hawaii residents, too. Your hotel, or the Hawaii Visitors Bureau, will have a complete listing. The daily papers are also good sources of information on what's coming up.

MONEY MATTERS

Currency: Foreign visitors should note that there are bills of $1, $2 (rare), $5, $10, $20, $50 and $100. Higher denominations are not in general circulation. All bills are the same shape and color so it might be difficult to tell them apart. The coins are 1 cent (penny), 5 cents (nickel), 10 cents (dime), 25 cents (quarter) and 50 cents (half-dollar) and the new $1 coin.

Banks and Currency Exchange: Most Hawaii banks are open from 8.30 a.m. to 3 p.m. Mondays through Fridays, though a few keep longer hours and operate on weekends (Oahu's airport currency-exchange office is open from 8:30 a.m. to 4:30 p.m. and 8 p.m. to 3 a.m.). Hotels provide information on currency-exchange hours, many exchanging foreign currency themselves, but not at very favorable rates.

Hawaii's shops, restaurants and other establishments do not, to all intents and purposes, accept foreign currency.

Credit Cards: Most hotels, restaurants, clothing stores, car rental agencies and other businesses accept major credit cards. Other proof of identification, such as a driver's license or passport may be required.

Traveler's Checks: Hotels, tour operators, shops and restaurants will accept traveler's checks drawn on American banks.

NEWSPAPERS and MAGAZINES. Some U.S. West Coast newspapers may be purchased in Honolulu, but they're often a day late and cost twice as much as on the U.S. Mainland because they are flown in.

Hawaii has two daily papers, the morning *Honolulu Advertiser* and the afternoon *Honolulu Star-Bulletin*. A wide range of magazines are available at newsstands and some bookstores. The monthly *Honolulu Magazine* prints a calendar of coming events.

A number of free tourist publications are brought out in Waikiki and a few on the Neighbor Islands as well. They range from newspaper-like tabloids to small booklets and their sole reason for being in business is the tourist. They keep up to date on what's going on—but be careful, because many of their tips are heavily oriented toward their advertisers.

PHOTOGRAPHY. Photographers will find breathtaking shots around every curve in Hawaii. Interisland travel via low-flying air taxis gives opportunities for particularly thrilling photography, and if the weather

P and other passengers agree, pilots often will take short detours to show even more scenic wonders.

All popular film makes and sizes are available. Overnight development is a specialty of many Waikiki shops.

POLICE. Despite what you may have seen on popular television series, there is no state police force in Hawaii. Each island has its own police force. In Honolulu, police officers wear navy-blue uniforms. They generally patrol in cars, unmarked except for a blue light on top, but there are also some blue-and-white marked ones. Motorcycle police patrol highways. In Waikiki, police have begun patrolling on foot.

In case of emergency on Oahu, Maui and Kauai, dial 911. For Hawaii Island, dial numbers listed in telephone book.

PUBLIC HOLIDAYS. The following are Hawaii State holidays and U.S. national holidays observed in Hawaii. Public offices and banks close on holidays, but shops are open on several of these:

January 1	New Year's Day
Third Monday in January	Martin Luther King Day
Third Monday in February	Presidents' Day
March 26	Prince Kuhio Day
Last Monday in May	Memorial Day
June 11	Kamehameha Day
July 4	Independence Day
Third Friday in August	Admission Day
First Monday in September	Labor Day
November 11	Veterans' Day
Fourth Thursday in November	Thanksgiving
December 25	Christmas Day

Moveable date: Good Friday.

R **RADIO and TV.** More than 20 radio stations compete with each other in Honolulu, catering to every taste in music.

Television stations broadcast practically around the clock. U.S. visitors will find most of their favorite shows are shown a week late and at different times of the day or night than on the Mainland. Network news is broadcast the same day, generally at 5:30 or 6 p.m., depending on the station. Many sports programs are broadcast live or via satellite daily.

RELIGIOUS SERVICES. A variety of religions is represented in Honolulu. Lists of churches can be found in most hotel lobbies, some hotels even having services on the premises. The Yellow Pages of the telephone directories also list churches and, in many instances, hours of services.

SIGHTSEEING HOURS. Hours may fluctuate, so best check first.

Big Island (Hawaii)

City of Refuge (Honaunau, Kona Coast): 8 a.m. to 5:30 p.m. daily.

Hulihee Palace (Kailua-Kona): 9 a.m. to 4 p.m. daily.

Lyman Mission House and Museum (Hilo): 10 a.m. to 4 p.m. Mondays through Saturdays.

Oahu

Bishop Museum (Honolulu): 9 a.m. to 5 p.m. daily, closed at Christmas.

Foster Botanical Gardens (Honolulu): 9 a.m. to 4 p.m. daily; free guided tours Mondays and Wednesdays at 1 p.m., closed Christmas and New Year.

Honolulu Academy of Arts: 10 a.m. to 4.30 p.m. Tuesday through Saturday, 1 to 5 p.m. Sunday, closed on Mondays and holidays.

Iolani Palace (Honolulu): 9 a.m. to 2:15 p.m. Wednesdays through Saturdays; tours every 15 minutes lasting 45 minutes. Closed Sundays through Tuesdays. By reservation only.

Mission Houses Museum (Honolulu): 9 a.m. to 4 p.m. Tuesday through Saturday, noon to 4 p.m. Sunday, closed Mondays and Thanksgiving, Christmas and New Year. Guided tours available.

Queen Emma's Summer Palace (Nuuanu Valley): 9 a.m. to 4 p.m. daily.

Sea Life Park (Makapuu Point, Waimanalo): 9:30 a.m. to 5 p.m. daily; continuous shows from 10:15 a.m.

Waikiki Aquarium: 9 a.m. to 5 p.m. daily.

TIME DIFFERENCES. Hawaii is on Hawaiian Standard Time all year round. The chart on p. 124 shows the time in various cities in winter.

Hawaii	Los Angeles	New York	London	Sydney	Auckland
noon Sunday	2 p.m. Sunday	5 p.m. Sunday	10 p.m. Sunday	9 a.m. Monday	11 a.m. Monday

To get the time, ring 983-3211.

TIPPING. Service is never included in restaurant bills. The usual tip is 15%. It's also appropriate to give something extra to bellboys, doormen, etc., for their services. The chart below gives some suggestions as to how much to leave.

Guide	10%
Hairdresser/Barber	15%
Hotel maid, per week	$3–5 (optional)
Porter, per bag	$1–2
Taxi driver	15%

TOILETS. Public toilets can be used in restaurants, department stores and office buildings, as well as on many public beaches, but because of vandalism they may not be in good shape. Toilets may be marked *Kane* for men and *Wahine* for women.

TOURIST INFORMATION OFFICES. The Hawaii Visitors Bureau in Honolulu, at 2270 Kalakaua Avenue (Suite 801, Waikiki Business Plaza, tel. 923-1811), is open from 8 a.m. to 4:30 p.m. Mondays through Fridays. Information about all the islands is available in Honolulu, but for more precise questions on the individual islands, consult the island office:

Hawaii (Big Island): Suite 105, Hilo Plaza, 180 Kinoole Street, Hilo. 75-5719 W. Alii Dr., Kailua-Kona.

Kanai: Suite 207, Luhue Plaza Building, 3016 Umi Street, Lihue.

Maui: Suite N16, 250 Alamaha Street, Kahului.

Other offices:

Chicago: Suite 2210, 180 North Michigan Avenue, IL 60601.

Los Angeles: Room 502, Central Plaza, 3440 Wilshire Boulevard, CA 90010.

New York: Room 1003, 441 Lexington Avenue, N.Y. 10017.

San Francisco: Suite 450, 50 California St., CA 94111.

UK: 14, The Green, Richmond, Surrey TW9 1PX.

Canada: 205-1624 56th Street, Delta, B.C. V4L 2B1.

TRANSPORTATION

Buses: Honolulu's bus service is excellent with connections between Waikiki and other parts of Honolulu, as well as around the island. Stops are marked with yellow-and-orange striped signs, and the same motif of yellow-and-orange stripes is picked up for the buses (called *TheBus*). Waikiki buses generally run from 5 a.m. to midnight. Buses on other routes usually start about 6 a.m. and stop earlier. Since it's possible to go by bus around most of Oahu, many visitors use the bus system for inexpensive sightseeing. A special guide, *Honolulu and Oahu by TheBus*, gives sensible itineraries for seeing the island in a relaxed way.

The city also operates a bus to Hanauma Bay and Sandy and Makapuu beaches as well as to Sea Life Park every half hour, and any Waikiki bus driver will tell you where to board them.

Persons aged 65 and older may apply for a free pass for bus travel, but it takes from 2 to 3 weeks for the passes to arrive.

The only other island with public bus service is Hawaii (Big Island), where buses are geared more to local residents' needs than visitors'. Some Neighbor Island resort areas, such as Kaanapali on Maui, run shuttle buses to shopping districts.

You can get schedule information on *TheBus* on Oahu by visiting the Bus Information Center at Ala Moana Shopping Center in Honolulu, or by phoning 848-5555.

Taxis: Taxis are not allowed to cruise in Honolulu except along bus routes after the buses have stopped running. There are stands at Ala Moana Shopping Center, in front of hotels and at the airport. Otherwise phone for a taxi.

WATER. The water is safe to drink. You may no longer automatically receive a glass of water when you sit down in a restaurant, but if you ask, you will be given one.

Index

An asterisk (*) next to a page number indicates a map reference.